I Heart Soul Food

I Heart Soul Food

100 SOUTHERN COMFORT FOOD FAVORITES

ROSIE MAYES

Photography and styling by
Michael and Danielle Kartes

SASQUATCH BOOKS
SEATTLE

This book is dedicated to my son, Giovanni. You are simply the best gift ever and the reason I live. I thank God every day for you. I am so lucky to be your mother! Also, a special thanks to Anthony for believing in me when no one else did.

I also want to dedicate this book to my online cousins on my blog, YouTube channel, Facebook, and Instagram.

Finally, last but not least, this book is dedicated to my grandpa Thomas Henderson. Thank you for being my father figure and molding me into a boss. I will always love you. —Baby

CONTENTS

◇◇◇◇◇◇◇◇◇◇◇◇◇◇◇◇◇◇◇◇◇◇◇◇◇◇

RECIPE LIST

THE STAR OF THE SOUL FOOD SUPPER

THE DESSERT TABLE

A LITTLE SOMETHING TO SIP

INTRODUCTION

◇◇

In the world I was born into, biscuit dough is the best toy, and children teethe on oxtail bones: soul food runs through my family tree like kudzu vines in the South. On my blog and YouTube channel, I Heart Recipes, and now in this book, I bring those Southern roots into my Seattle kitchen and share everything my mom taught me, everything my grandmother taught her, and all of my inherited, long-nurtured love of soul food with the world.

I was just three or four years old when my aunt Frances first brought me into the kitchen, plopped me on a stool, and let my chubby little baby fingers dig into the flour, salt, and spices while she cooked. I patted the pork chops through the breading, following her on how much I needed of each ingredient, then handed them over to her to deep-fry. It was the first time I cooked soul food, but it certainly wasn't the first time I ate it, and it was only the beginning of my lifelong love of making the kind of food that sticks to your ribs and warms your heart.

From the moment I could walk, I followed my mom along with her mom and sisters to the Parkside Nursing Home in Seattle's Capitol Hill neighborhood, where they whipped up grand batches of macaroni and cheese, meatloaf, and gumbo for the residents, and I took the scraps they handed me and mimicked their actions, building my own pretend dishes in a corner of the commercial kitchen. It was probably illegal, and I know they wouldn't let you do that kind of thing today, but there was nowhere else for me to go while they worked—and nowhere I loved to be more than making trouble at their feet as the smells of soul food wafted around us.

By the time I was five, I stepped up to the stove to make real food, cooking up a big ol' batch of my favorite spaghetti, and that became my dish. Everyone in the family has something they're known for—my mom's is her potato salad—that they always have to bring to family picnics and holiday parties. I still make my spaghetti just the same way, and it still brings the same Southern mentality to my Pacific Northwest kitchen, just like it did when I wasn't even tall enough to stir the sauce without a little bit of help.

Because even though I was born and raised in Seattle, my cooking is firmly rooted in Baton Rouge, Louisiana. My grandma—my mom's mom—and her husband, my grandfather, left Baton Rouge during the Great Migration and headed north for a better life, pregnant with the first of what would be eighteen children. (Yeah, you read that right—eighteen kids. That's why I've got so many aunts that made sure I knew how to cook!) My grandma found that better life in Seattle, where my mom was born the youngest of the six girls, along with twelve brothers, and my grandmother took over as the queen bee of an always-busy kitchen. When those kids grew up, they all had a few kids of their own—that's why I'm always known as Cousin Rosie—and she fed them too. She never lost her role as a Southern belle, whipping out Creole and Cajun cooking that fed her family's heart and soul (and a lot of the neighbors too) and kept them remembering where they came from.

With a giant family like that, every gathering was an event. Sunday supper always drew a crowd, and there was never any shortage of hungry mouths, so anyone who wanted to cook a dish was always welcome to step into the kitchen. But there was one day of the year that took even our family's big appetites beyond their wildest dreams.

Christmas with my family was the biggest, most delicious celebration you've ever seen. We would have a turkey, a ham, *and* a giant pot of gumbo on the table. There were collard greens, candied yams, and my mom's famous potato salad, which might be the best ever—except for mine! There were cornbread rolls and my grandma's special fried chicken made with waffle batter. But the best part was dessert. Or, rather, all the desserts. See, my grandparents didn't have much money, and they couldn't possibly afford gifts for all those children, so the present was the Christmas dessert table. By the time the next generation rolled in—my cousins and me—the tradition had solidified, and anything less than every dessert imaginable would have let the crowd down. Buttermilk chocolate cake, sweet potato pie, peach cobbler, pineapple upside-down cake, and tea cakes (those were my great-grandmother's recipe—she wasn't a great cook, but she made these so well that nothing else mattered) all spilled over the top of a table in the living room. It was a sweet feast that seemed to have no end.

My beloved grandma died when I was only two, but I carry on her legacy as a cook in my kitchen and in my name: she was Rosa Mae, and I was named Rosemary after her. Funny, the name Mayes actually came from my husband, though! I grew up eating the recipes she'd passed on to her daughters and was somehow the only kid in my generation that dared to step into the kitchen (though you better believe my cousins call me up when they need a taste of home). Her husband, my grandfather, cared for me and raised me on photos and stories of my namesake and the wonders that came from her oven and stove. There was never any question that I would follow in her footsteps, right into the kitchen.

The recipes were never written down, though, so by the time I grew up and tried to make all the dishes I'd heard of, I had only tidbits and lessons passed on by aunts and tastes nabbed at family reunions back in Baton Rouge. So I started recording them, recreating each recipe, making them over and over in the kitchen until they matched my memory of them—and the uncles and aunts all gave them the thumbs-up. Then I would share them with my online audience.

See, I was lucky that pieces of all of these delicious Southern, Creole, and Cajun recipes trickled down to me. You name it—gumbo, smothered chicken, collard greens, sweet cornbread—I make it all. But at some point, I noticed that a lot of my friends didn't know their way around the kitchen. They never patted biscuit dough on the corner of the counter at the Parkside. They weren't fortunate enough to get their grandmother's oxtail recipes from their mom or to learn to fry pork chops with their aunt Frances. So I became the friend and cousin that everyone called for help—the Butterball-turkey helpline for year-round soul food assistance, Cousin Rosie here to help.

Meanwhile, around 2009, I was getting a bit burnt out with my work as a patient care technician and certified nursing assistant. I'd been at the same place, doing end-of-life care for five years, and I was emotionally wrung out. I worked twelve hours a day, had a young son, and didn't do much for myself. "You need a hobby," my husband suggested. (He was right.) On my birthday, I was bored and he had to work. And so, in a move I had no idea how much would change my life, I turned a camera on myself and started a video blog. At first it was a mishmash of all things I was good at—an online diary pep-pered with makeup tips and tutorials or long monologues about whatever was on my mind. Then one day, I decided to record myself making dinner.

I made fried chicken, macaroni and cheese, and peas. My brother came over (he's always over if there's fried chicken around) and recorded it on his girlfriend's brand-new camera. When I posted it on my video channel at the time, it went nuts.

It all made perfect sense. There weren't a lot of soul food blogs out there—it was almost like soul food didn't exist online. There were baking blogs everywhere, seventeen million different diet blogs, and all sorts of niches that were filled, but not this one. I knew that there had to be an audience for authentic soul food recipes—and that first video proved it. I just needed to call on the lessons that my mom, her sisters, and—indirectly—my grandma had taught me, and I could put that all to good use.

I created my blog and YouTube channel and focused on Southern and soul food. The first five years that I had them, I was juggling the blog and channel with my full-time job. But then big companies started looking for my videos, and people wanted to pay me for what I had created out of my love for my food roots. They saw what I was doing and knew it was a worthwhile investment. It was all a bit of fate mixed with luck, kind of a total accident that changed my life.

Still, I wasn't going to complain about it—I was going to jump in with both feet. In 2014 I decided to take a leap of faith and quit my full-time job to start blogging as a career. Since then I've gained a lot of online family members via YouTube, my blog at IHeartRecipes.com, Facebook, Pinterest, and even Instagram. My family was big to start with, but my following makes even my seventeen aunts and uncles and their families look small in comparison.

And that's why I'm always Cousin Rosie—online and in person—and I'm still sharing old-fashioned, authentic soul food like my grandma made, along with anything else that I can cook up. I find recipe inspiration everywhere and anywhere I go.

I love to eat, so if I have something at a restaurant that I like, I want to re-create it at home—you'll see favorites from places I grew up on, like the Blueberry Cornbread Waffles on page 23. Or when I've got a craving, I have to figure out what's going to satisfy it (usually it involves one of my many variations on macaroni and cheese). I come up with a lot of ideas on my own, but also my subscribers and fans constantly email me or write to me on social media asking for recipes. I'm eager to please and want to make

sure that everybody is fed, just like my grandma did, so if there's something I don't have a recipe for yet, I just play around in the kitchen until I come up with the perfect one. But I always put my Cousin Rosie spin on it—whether that's adding a Cajun or Creole touch to it, making it easier with modern appliances, or adding a totally unexpected ingredient, because I heart (creating) recipes!

What Is Soul Food?

My cooking comes from the Southern American tradition, from the places where my grandmother and grandfather grew up, namely Baton Rouge, Louisiana. But I'm not from the South; I grew up in Seattle, in the Pacific Northwest, so I don't like to call my food Southern food. Instead, I call it soul food. It includes the Jamaican food that my great-grandmother ate and the seafood-centric dishes that I make from the great stuff that's available in the Pacific Northwest. But it's all soul food because I use what I have and I put my all into it; I'm serving love on a plate. And that love is mostly made of seasoning salt—garlic powder, onion powder, and a little bit of paprika for color.

STOCKING THE SOUL FOOD KITCHEN

◇◇◇◇◇◇◇◇◇◇◇◇◇◇◇◇◇◇◇◇◇◇◇

I like to cook from what I have on hand—to make something out of nothing—so every time I consider what to make, the first step is to open the pantry. Whoa. It's overwhelming in there!

The key to cooking like this is to have a well-stocked pantry. Mine tends to be overflowing because when I grocery shop, I buy whatever I see that looks good; whatever pops into my head, that's what I put in the cart—especially in my favorite aisles: the seafood and baking ones.

This style works for me because I've got a soul food pantry on hand, with shelf after shelf of all my favorite ingredients, and a kitchen full of the equipment needed to cook it all. If you don't, I'm here to help: I put together this list to help you get stocked up and ready to cook your way through the book.

I suggest a few of my favorite brands for some products, but don't feel like you have to get the exact ones—soul food is all about making do with what you can find easily and what you can afford. Don't skip something on sale just because it's not what Cousin Rosie listed. In fact, I'm all about substituting for what you have on hand or what suits your personal tastes.

Are y'all ready to get started in the kitchen? To cook from the soul and serve love on the plate, you need plenty of spices, herbs, and always—as anyone who's seen my videos knows—a little bit of paprika for color.

A LOOK IN MY PANTRY

Spice It Up

Bay leaves: Nobody can ever explain what bay leaves do, but they just sort of make everything taste better! You can't skip them in your gumbo or jambalaya.

Black pepper (ground, coarse, and cracked): Black pepper is an essential piece of the soul food flavor puzzle, and I use it in three different sizes of grind throughout the book. If you have a pepper grinder, you can do this yourself by twisting the grinder—ground will be almost a powder, fine enough to disappear into dishes; coarse, a little bit bigger so that you can see it in salad dressings and such; and cracked pepper is bigger, almost like peppercorn flakes, and will add texture and be visible at the end of the dish.

Cajun seasoning: The base is similar to Creole seasoning, but Cajun food loves spice, so it's also got red pepper, cayenne pepper, and white pepper. My favorite brand is called Tone's.

Creole seasoning: This is similar to seasoning salt, but with the addition of a few herbs and spices—you can make it yourself, but I just buy Tony Chachere's; it works for my gumbo (and so much more).

Garlic powder: Along with fresh garlic, the powder creates layers of flavors in many soul food dishes.

Kosher salt: All my recipes are tested with kosher salt—it's the standard for cooking with.

Lemon pepper: I love the convenience of this mix of lemon oil, salt, and black pepper that I buy from McCormick to use on my chicken, seafood, and pork.

Old Bay Seasoning: This is a classic seafood seasoning. I always mix it into the cornmeal and flour for fried seafood, or shake it directly onto shrimp or lobster.

Onion powder: The powerful, savory flavor of onion powder will punch up any boring dish.

Paprika: Few dishes are complete without the stunning dots of red that come from paprika.

Parsley flakes: I have to have some color (like paprika), and the green of this dried herb lights up any dark stews or beans.

Poultry seasoning: Another McCormick favorite, this mix of thyme, sage, and other herby flavors always finds its way onto my chicken and turkey.

Red pepper flakes: I can't help it—I just always want to add red pepper flakes to give a little kick to a dish.

Seasoning salt: I make my own version, mixing kosher salt, garlic powder, onion powder, black pepper, and a little paprika (for color), but if you'd rather buy some, my favorite kind is Johnny's.

Thyme: I typically use dried herbs over fresh because they are cheap and don't go bad—which is good because I need plenty of thyme for all of my bean dishes!

Bake It Better

All-purpose flour: As the name implies, this flour does everything—baking, frying, and even thickening gravies. I prefer the Pillsbury version.

Baking soda and baking powder: These are leavening agents, so you'll need them to make sure your baked goods rise. Any kind will work, as long as they're not too old—they lose their power over time.

Baking spray: Baker's Joy makes sliding your baked goods out of the pan so much easier—it's a mix of oil and flour without the mess of greasing a pan and then dusting it.

Brown sugar: I use brown sugar (either dark or light) in most of my desserts, but I'll also sneak it into red sauces to bring down the acidity.

Cake flour: Finer than all-purpose flour, cake flour makes my cakes lighter and fluffier. Before I got really into baking, my grandmother-in-law tipped me off that Swans Down is the best, so that's what I try to have on hand.

Cornmeal: I use Albers yellow cornmeal, which is finely ground, because that's what my mom and her mom before her used, so I know it makes my cornbread and breading for seafood just how I like it.

Cornstarch: Buy whatever brand is on sale, but you will want to have this around to thicken gravies and dessert fillings.

Granulated sugar: This is just regular white sugar—everything needs a little sweetness. I usually buy C&H brand for all my sugars.

Nonstick cooking spray: Spray cans make greasing things way easier—it's just oil, but easier. I use PAM.

Powdered sugar: You need this on hand for baking to create icings and frostings for all those fabulous desserts—and to top your waffles and French toast!

Self-rising flour: I reach for this premade mix (it has baking powder and salt in it) when making biscuits, but I also love it for any kind of frying because it helps make stuff come out extra crispy. If you can't find it, you can make your own with 1 cup all-purpose flour plus 1½ teaspoons baking powder and ¼ teaspoon fine kosher salt.

Vanilla extract: This is a baking essential, but it can get really expensive, so I like to buy the Kirkland Signature brand at Costco or whatever is on sale. It's just important to make sure that it's pure vanilla, not imitation, because it does taste different.

Fatten Up That Fridge

Butter (salted and unsalted): My grandmother always used Darigold butter, a local company here in the Northwest, so it's what I use. And though many people avoid salted butter in baking, I use it there too because I like salt. If you don't like it as much, use unsalted and add salt to your taste.

Buttermilk: I love using buttermilk in desserts, like my Buttermilk Chocolate Cake on page 206. If you can't find it, make it yourself by stirring a tablespoon of lemon juice or distilled white vinegar into a cup of milk and letting it stand for ten minutes.

Cheese: My favorite cheeses are sharp cheddar and Havarti—you'll see them over and over in my recipes, along with a few others. I mostly pick up the Boar's Head brand.

Eggs: When I call for eggs, I mean large—it's what I buy (the store brand is fine: I go through a lot, and I need them to be affordable).

Half-and-half: This is just a mix of heavy cream and milk, so if you don't have it on hand, just mix them one-to-one.

Heavy cream: This is an essential for baking and making frosting.

Milk: It's important to always use whole milk in the recipes, no low-fat stuff here.

Savory Essentials

Bell peppers: I like really dark-green or red bell peppers.

Broth and stock: I simply do not have the time to be making all the broths and stocks that I use in my kitchen. I buy vegetable broth (for greens dishes), beef broth (for oxtails and roasts), and chicken broth (for most everything else), as well as seafood stock for my gumbo and the like.

Canned tomatoes: For spaghetti, I'll need tomatoes to make that red sauce. But I also add them to stews, and my Louisiana family members say I'm weird, but I like them in my gumbo.

Dry beans: I've always got pinto beans to cook up with ham hocks and red beans to cook with stronger flavors like sausage and smoked turkey.

Garlic: I love garlic. I usually have fresh garlic on hand, but I always have preminced garlic as well.

Green onions: The fattest stems and the brightest colors bring the best flavor.

Ketchup: It's a condiment, but you want to keep enough around to cook with it too. Either way, I stick to the standard Heinz.

Mayonnaise: Everybody has a favorite mayonnaise based on what they grew up with. For me, that's Hellmann's/Best Foods. If you have a different favorite, that's okay—use that.

Mustard: When I say mustard, I'm talking about the throwback, classic standard yellow stuff from French's, nothing fancy.

Olive oil: Olive is the best oil for sautéing vegetables and dressing salads, and I especially like the kind from the Oilerie, which can be found online.

Pasta: I make a lot of macaroni and cheese and spaghetti, so I always have elbows and spaghetti noodles on hand. I never know if someone's going to stop by, and I can whip those up in a second.

Potatoes: Russet potatoes are cheap and work in all my potato dishes. I stick to the medium size because they're easy to peel and cut.

Vegetable oil: I mostly use Mazola corn oil because it's what my mom and aunts use, especially for deep-frying, but I switch to canola for baking.

White rice: Rice is mostly a filler in my kitchen, so the type is not super important, but it should be long grain.

Worcestershire sauce: This is a key ingredient to add a little saltiness and flavor to dishes.

Yellow and red onions: I use yellow onions—my favorite is our local Walla Walla variety—and big shiny red onions. I look for ones where the peel is a bit broken so I can see that they're not brown inside.

ALL MY TOOLS

I cook soul food, so my kitchen is pretty bare-bones. There are a few appliances that I love because they make my life easier and my cleanup process simpler—like my beloved deep fryer—but for the most part, this is just a list of what I keep in my kitchen. I cook the way I do because I'm always looking for what's quick, affordable, and not too complicated—and most of that comes from how I cook, not what sort of tools I'm using.

9-by-13-inch baking dish: The clear Pyrex type is my go-to baking dish, but sometimes I'll bake a lasagna or something in a nicer casserole dish if I'm bringing it to a party. An oval baking dish works just as well as rectangular, as long as it holds similar volume.

Aluminum foil: Since baking dishes don't usually come with oven-safe tops, I use foil when I need to cover the food when it's in the oven.

Colander: Obviously, you need a colander to drain your pasta, but they're also great for rinsing vegetables.

Deep fryer: One place I do have a strong opinion is the deep fryer. I use a Hamilton Beach 12-cup capacity with a basket. It heats up fast, I can drop a lot of food in at once, I don't have to fish around for pieces of food in the oil, and it's easy to clean. If you don't have a deep fryer, I recommend that you use a 12-inch cast-iron pan and a candy/deep-fry thermometer to measure your temperatures.

Dry measuring cups: Cheap steel handheld measuring cups work great and are better than plastic because the measurements are etched in, rather than printed, so they don't wear off.

Dutch oven: If something has to go from the stove top to the oven, my cast-iron Dutch oven works for both and reduces extra dishes to wash.

Grill pan: I like to use my grill pans for steaks and grilled seafood.

Handheld mixer: I use my handheld mixer for almost everything because it's easy to clean up afterward. Mine is a KitchenAid because I like all the attachments for it, like the dough hooks.

Kitchen shears: Knives scare me, so I use my kitchen shears to break down a whole raw chicken instead.

Large Bundt pan: This is what I use to make my pound cakes and angel food cakes. If it's not nonstick, you'll want to use baking spray.

Large pot: I've got an aluminum Calphalon and a stainless-steel Cuisinart pot, and I use whichever is closest when I boil pasta or make gumbo.

Liquid measuring cups: I use my two-cup Pyrex measuring cup for almost everything.

Masher: I use the kind of masher where the bottom looks like a squiggly line—but you can also mash with a whisk if you don't have a masher.

Measuring spoons: Like the measuring cups, I prefer the steel and in a range from ⅛ teaspoon to 1 tablespoon. I don't like the ones that say "a pinch." That's not a specific amount!

Mixing bowls: I like to use glass mixing bowls so I can see what I'm doing—if there's any spots or clumps that I missed.

Paring knife: Remember how I don't like knives? I pretty much use only my little paring knife for everything—and kitchen shears for anything else.

Potato peeler: Whatever kind of peeler you have works, though I prefer the long, thin kind—and always with the bit at the end to pull out the eyes.

Round cake pans: I use 9-inch Wilton cake pans; they usually come in a set of two for layer cakes.

Saucepan: My 12-inch nonstick is my everyday go-to pan.

Sifter: Sifting takes the lumps out of flour before you use it, but if you don't have a sifter, you can just use your whisk to do the same thing.

Slow cooker: My slow cooker is a workhorse: I just throw everything in and don't have to babysit it. It's a Crock-Pot brand, just like my mom had, but the digital version so I can just set a timer and then it turns to warm. Make sure that you are familiar with your slow cooker! Old slow cookers tend to run a tad bit hotter than newer ones, and this can affect your cooking time.

Spatula: Anything goes here, except for metal, which will scratch your nonstick pans. I prefer wood, but plastic is good too.

Springform pan: A high-quality nonstick springform pan is an essential for making cheesecake.

Stand mixer: I use my stand mixer mostly for big cakes or holidays. It's also a KitchenAid, and I like the tilt-head kind more than the bowl-lift, as it's easier to remove the bowl and clean.

Tongs: I use all-metal tongs for flipping things when I'm frying.

Whisk: In a whisk, metal is the best way to go.

Wooden spoons: Wood doesn't scratch my pots, and if you care for them properly, they last a long time. Be sure to wash your wooden spoons by hand, and dry immediately.

Starting the Day with Soul

Blueberry Cornbread Waffles

These waffles are a combination of my son's two favorite foods (waffles and cornbread) and one of mine (blueberries). When I was growing up, we used to sometimes go out to breakfast at a local restaurant near my hometown of Seattle and get them. While the restaurant still exists, which is amazing, it has changed over the years and sadly no longer makes the most important dish on the menu, at least to me. I missed the heartiness that the cornmeal adds to the batter and the dots of blue from the fruit embedded inside, so I took the idea into my own kitchen and figured out just how they made them. I serve these piled up with all my favorite toppings, all at once: butter, whipped cream, fresh blueberries, and maple syrup.

MAKES 4 TO 6 SERVINGS

1½ cup all-purpose flour	1¼ cups buttermilk
½ cup yellow cornmeal	2 eggs, lightly beaten
¼ cup granulated sugar	½ cup (1 stick) unsalted butter, melted
½ teaspoon kosher salt	¾ cup frozen blueberries, thawed
1½ teaspoon baking powder	

◆ Preheat your waffle iron.

◆ In a large mixing bowl, combine the flour, cornmeal, sugar, salt, and baking powder. Mix the dry ingredients until well combined.

◆ In the center of the dry ingredients, make a small well. Add in the buttermilk, eggs, and melted butter. Mix with a whisk until well combined. Then fold the blueberries into the batter.

◆ Spray the waffle iron with nonstick cooking spray. Place 1 to 1½ cups of batter onto the iron, and cook until the outer parts are nice and crisp. Repeat until there is no more batter. Serve and enjoy with your favorite toppings.

Banana Nut Pancakes

My mom and my grandpa always had bananas on hand. I remember sitting at the breakfast table while my grandpa sliced them up over his cornflakes every morning, and my mom would always bake hers into banana bread. But if there were a few ripe bananas hanging out when the weekend rolled around, I would always request that she make them into banana nut pancakes for breakfast.

Now that I'm all grown up, I can make them whenever I want, which is useful because I don't eat bananas as often as my grandfather did, so sometimes I have a few that I need to use up before they're going to get tossed. While my mom always relied on a baking mix for hers, I prefer to make my pancakes from scratch. Then I'm able to truly customize the pancakes to my liking—and I've got a serious sweet tooth, so that means I can add as much sugar as I want! I also like to add a nice amount of cinnamon and vanilla to my batter, and it really makes these pancakes pop. Once they're cooked, I always pile on extra banana slices, add whipped cream, sprinkle a few more chopped pecans on, and then pour maple syrup over the top.

MAKES 6 TO 10 SERVINGS

1 cup all-purpose flour	1 cup buttermilk
2 tablespoons dark brown sugar	1 egg, lightly beaten
1 teaspoon baking powder	2 tablespoons unsalted butter, melted
½ teaspoon baking soda	
1 teaspoon ground cinnamon	2 teaspoons vanilla extract
½ teaspoon ground nutmeg	¼ cup chopped pecans
½ teaspoon kosher salt	Vegetable oil, for the skillet
1 large ripe banana, mashed	

* In a large bowl, combine the flour, sugar, baking powder, baking soda, cinnamon, nutmeg, and salt. Whisk until everything is well combined, then set the bowl to the side.

* Next, in a separate medium bowl, combine the mashed banana, buttermilk, egg, melted butter, and vanilla. Mix the ingredients using a handheld mixer until incorporated.

- Make a small well in the center of the dry ingredients, and pour the wet ingredients in. Use a handheld mixer to mix the ingredients again. Sprinkle in the pecans, then fold into the batter. Set the bowl to the side.

- Lightly oil a medium-size skillet and place it over medium heat. When the skillet is hot, pour in about ½ cup of the pancake batter. Cook until the edges are golden and bubbles have formed, about 2 minutes. Flip the pancake and cook for 2 more minutes. Repeat until there is no more batter. Serve and enjoy with your favorite toppings.

Ultimate French Toast

Everybody loves French toast, but I find the standard version that you usually get at restaurants to be a little boring, so I made a few little tweaks, making for a way better breakfast.

First, I like to start with something called French toast bread. Look for it at the store. Then I make sure I use thick slices—and I never pat them when they're cooking or that lovely fluffiness will disappear. Finally, I mix both brown and granulated sugar into my batter, along with cinnamon, nutmeg, and lots of vanilla to really kick up the flavor. These simple additions totally change the game.

I like to top mine with a little more melted butter, then sprinkle with powdered sugar and drizzle with maple syrup.

MAKES 12 SERVINGS

3 eggs	2 teaspoons ground cinnamon
2 cups whole milk	¼ teaspoon ground nutmeg
1 tablespoon brown sugar	¼ cup unsalted butter, melted
1 tablespoon granulated sugar	12 slices French toast bread or
2 teaspoons vanilla extract	thick-sliced bread

◆ In large bowl or dish, crack open the eggs and beat them. Pour in the milk and add the sugars, vanilla, cinnamon, and nutmeg. Stir to combine, then pour in the melted butter and stir again.

◆ Start adding 1 to 2 bread slices at a time to the milk-and-egg mixture. Let each slice stay in the wet mixture for about 10 seconds.

◆ Spray your large skillet or griddle with nonstick cooking spray and place it over medium heat. Once the skillet/griddle is hot, add the bread 2 to 4 slices at a time. Cook each side of the bread until it is nice and golden brown. Serve immediately with butter, syrup, powdered sugar, or your favorite toppings.

Caramel Pecan Cinnamon Rolls

Every time I make these, I can hear people whispering—they are always worried there won't be enough! But they are big and fluffy, and I always make sure to make more rolls than there are people, because the light, soft texture from the cake flour means that some hungry folks will want more. They pair well with a hot cup of coffee and a few slices of crisp bacon, especially on a slow, cool morning.

MAKES 8 TO 12 ROLLS

For the dough:
½ cup warm water
0.75-ounce package (6¾ teaspoons) fast-acting yeast
2 tablespoons plus 1 teaspoon granulated sugar, divided
5 ounces evaporated milk, warm
5 tablespoons vegetable oil, plus more for the bowl
1 egg, beaten
1 tablespoon vanilla extract
1 teaspoon kosher salt
4½ cups cake flour

For the filling:
1¼ cups (2½ sticks) unsalted butter, at room temperature, plus more for greasing

½ cup brown sugar
¼ cup granulated sugar
1 teaspoon ground cinnamon
½ teaspoon ground nutmeg

For the icing:
2 tablespoons unsalted butter, at room temperature
2 ounces cream cheese, at room temperature
3 tablespoons whole milk
2 teaspoons vanilla extract
3 cups powdered sugar

Toppings:
½ cup chopped pecans
½ to ¾ cup caramel sauce, store-bought

CONTINUED

- Pour the warm water into a large mixing bowl or the bowl of a stand mixer, then sprinkle in the yeast and 1 teaspoon of the sugar. Mix until well combined, then let sit for about 7 minutes or until the yeast foams.

- Next, pour in the warm evaporated milk and stir. Add in the vegetable oil, egg, vanilla, salt, and the remaining 2 tablespoons sugar. Mix the ingredients on low speed using a handheld or stand mixer with the paddle attachment.

- Remove the mixing blade and replace with the dough hook. With the mixer on low speed, slowly start adding in the flour, about ¼ cup at a time. Once the dough has formed, remove it from the bowl and set to the side. Lightly oil the bowl, then return the dough to it and cover with a clean towel. Put the dough in a warm place and let rest for 1½ hours.

- After the dough has rested, punch the middle of the dough to remove air. Remove the dough from the bowl, and transfer to a lightly floured countertop. Flatten the dough using a rolling pin.

- In a large bowl, combine the butter, sugars, cinnamon, and nutmeg. Mix until well combined, then slather the butter mixture on top of the dough. Roll up the dough, then cut into 8 to 12 rolls.

- Lightly butter a 9-by-13-inch baking dish, then add in the rolls, leaving an inch between each one. Drape a clean towel over the dish, and let the rolls sit for 45 minutes. After the time has passed, uncover the rolls. At this point, the rolls should have increased in size and should be touching.

- Preheat oven to 375 degrees F.

- Bake the rolls for 15 to 20 minutes. Remove from the oven and let cool.

- In a medium bowl, combine the butter and cream cheese, and mix well using a handheld mixer. Add in the milk and vanilla, and stir to combine. Then add in the powdered sugar, and mix until creamy.

- Drizzle on the icing and caramel sauce, then sprinkle the pecans onto the rolls, Serve and enjoy!

Sweet Potato Biscuits

When you think of the traditional soul food breakfast, you probably picture one with buttery biscuits. Sometimes I like to try to improve on a classic: like these ultra-moist sweet potato biscuits in place of the standard white-flour ones.

I don't use a ton of sweet potato, just enough to add a tiny bit of color and sweetness. Just don't skip the step of putting them into the fridge, no matter how impatient you get—that cool rest will ensure they come out super flaky.

When they're done, I serve them with honey and butter for a weekend brunch, but I always like to stash a few away in the refrigerator for a quick weekday breakfast—just pop them into the microwave for 10 to 15 seconds.

MAKES 10 TO 12 BISCUITS

2 cups self-rising flour
1 tablespoon granulated sugar
½ teaspoon cream of tartar
⅛ teaspoon kosher salt

½ cup (1 stick) cold unsalted butter,
   shredded (with a cheese grater),
   plus more to top the cooked biscuits
½ cup mashed sweet potatoes
¾ cup buttermilk, cold
Vegetable oil, for greasing

- Preheat the oven to 400 degrees F.

- In a large mixing bowl or the bowl of a stand mixer, combine the flour, sugar, cream of tartar, and salt. Sift or whisk the ingredients until well combined. Add in the butter and mashed sweet potatoes, and mix on medium speed, using a handheld or stand mixer, for about 2 minutes. Slowly start pouring in the buttermilk with the mixer on medium speed. Mix until incorporated.

- Once the dough has formed, remove it from the bowl and flatten it out a bit (make sure it's about 1½ inches thick) on a lightly floured surface using a rolling pin. Cut the dough into 10 or 12 pieces.

- Lightly oil a 9-by-13-inch baking dish and place the biscuits in the dish, leaving a small space between each biscuit. Place the biscuits in the refrigerator for 10 minutes to get the dough nice and cold.

- Remove from the refrigerator and bake the biscuits for 12 to 15 minutes, or until they start to brown. Once done, brush butter on top of the biscuits while they are still warm. Serve and enjoy!

Shrimp, Andouille Sausage, and Grits

◇◇

I grew up on what I thought were the Southern classics—we had shrimp and grits, and we had sausage and grits. But when I was down in Baton Rouge for a family reunion, one of my older cousins made me a shrimp and grits that I couldn't believe. Playing around in the kitchen—I must have made this at least a half dozen times to figure it out—I realized that the Southern secret was combining the shrimp and grits with andouille sausage.

I start by making the grits first as those will take the longest (I use the Creamy Cheesy Grits on page 48 if I am feeling like a real bowl of comfort), then I pour the hot shrimp and sausage over the top just before serving.

MAKES 4 SERVINGS

3 cups water
2 teaspoons kosher salt
¾ cup quick grits
2 tablespoons extra-virgin olive oil
½ pound andouille sausage, cut into
  ½-inch-thick slices
½ pound large raw shrimp, peeled
  and deveined

1 teaspoon minced garlic
¼ cup chopped green onions, plus
  more for garnish
2 teaspoons Cajun seasoning
½ teaspoon ground black pepper
3 tablespoons salted butter

◆ In a medium saucepan over high heat, pour in the water and salt. Once the liquid starts to boil, immediately turn the heat down to medium. Stir the liquid, and gradually sprinkle in the grits. Let the grits cook until they thicken and get nice and creamy (usually 30 to 35 minutes), and be sure to stir frequently.

◆ While the grits are cooking, grab a pan and drizzle in the olive oil. Heat the oil up over medium-high heat, then toss in the andouille sausage. Cook for 5 to 7 minutes, or until it browns, then toss in the shrimp, garlic, and green onions. Sprinkle in the Cajun seasoning and black pepper.

◆ Cook for 5 more minutes, then turn off the heat. Once the grits have thickened, add in the butter and stir.

◆ Plate the grits, then add the sausage, shrimp, and onions on top. Garnish with extra green onions.

Beef Brisket Hash

<><><><><><><><><><><><><><><><><><><><><><><><><><><>

When I first started making my Slow Cooker Beef Brisket (page 146), it made enough for about twelve people, and we were only a family of three. That meant I had to get creative with how I used up the leftovers all week long—and with hash browns, bacon, and onions, we could eat this hash for days with toast and eggs. Now, my neighbors and cousins have learned about my brisket, so if I'm cooking it, they are knocking that door down. That means there's no more leftovers, and while I don't miss having to think up ways to use it up all week, I do try to sneak just enough off to the side so that I can make this dish—it's such a quick and easy shortcut to a filling weekday breakfast.

MAKES 6 SERVINGS

6 strips thick-cut bacon	2 cups chopped beef brisket
¼ cup vegetable oil	(page 146)
2¾ cups frozen hash browns, thawed	1 teaspoon garlic powder
1 medium red bell pepper, diced	1 teaspoon kosher salt
1 large yellow onion, diced	½ teaspoon ground black pepper
	¼ cup chopped green onions

◆ Place a large skillet over medium heat, then add in the bacon. Cook the bacon for about 5 minutes, or until it's nice and crisp. Remove the bacon from the skillet, but leave the rendered fat. Set the bacon to the side to cool.

◆ Add the vegetable oil to the skillet, and let it heat up over medium heat. Once the oil is nice and hot, add in the hash browns. Cook the potatoes until they are golden and tender, usually about 7 minutes.

◆ Add in the peppers and onions. Cook for 5 minutes. Then toss in the chopped beef brisket and sprinkle in the garlic powder, salt, and pepper. Stir the ingredients, and let cook for 7 more minutes.

◆ Crumble the bacon that you cooked earlier, and toss it in the skillet along with the green onions. Mix the ingredients, and turn off the heat. Serve and enjoy with your favorite breakfast sides.

Cajun Breakfast Burritos

I love breakfast burritos because they're quick and easy to eat on the go. But my Cajun country tastes mean that a lot of the burritos you see out there are a little bland for me, so I gave these a little South Louisiana makeover with plenty of salt and spice from the andouille sausage. When I used to work full-time, I'd prepare them on my day off and keep my freezer stocked with them so I could just warm them up and run off.

MAKES 6 SERVINGS

2 tablespoons vegetable oil
1 pound andouille sausage, diced
1 cup frozen hash browns, thawed
1 large red bell pepper, diced
½ medium red onion, diced

7 eggs, beaten
½ cup shredded cheddar cheese
½ cup shredded pepper jack cheese
6 large flour tortillas, warmed

◆ Set a large nonstick or well-seasoned cast-iron pan over medium heat, and drizzle in the vegetable oil. When the oil is hot, toss the sausage into the pan and cook until it slightly browns.

◆ Next, add in the hash browns, peppers, and onions. Cook everything for 4 to 5 minutes, or until it is tender. Remove the ingredients from the pan.

◆ Pour the eggs into the same pan and cook to desired doneness, then remove the eggs from the pan. Turn off the heat.

◆ In a large bowl, combine the eggs with the other ingredients. Sprinkle in the cheese and stir.

◆ Lay the warm tortillas on a flat surface, and add ½ cup of the filling on top of each. Roll up the tortillas, serve, and enjoy!

Note: To freeze the burritos, lay down aluminum foil, then add parchment paper on top of the foil. Place the burrito on top of the parchment paper, then wrap.

To warm up, thaw the burritos, then warm up in the oven at 350 degrees F for 10 to 15 minutes.

Chicken Fried Steak with Sausage Gravy

◇◇

If you think the name of this dish is confusing, you're not alone. Some people think it actually came out of a mistake a cook made at a restaurant, confusing two orders and mashing them into one. But just to be clear, this is a steak dish, and the name refers to the fact that we fry it just like we do chicken. Or, rather, usually a restaurant does the frying—that's where I'd always eaten it growing up.

Then one day, I was watching a cooking show and they made a version, and I thought, "Wait, why don't I make this myself?" Because I knew that with my own seasonings, homemade sausage gravy, and my trusty deep fryer, I could do even better.

This takes a little while to make, so it's usually a Sunday kind of meal, cooked up for a big weekend breakfast. I use cornstarch to get my breading shatteringly crisp and self-rising flour to keep it light and fluffy until it gets buried under the creamy gravy. I usually serve it with eggs and my Creamy Cheesy Grits (page 48) so that I have even more stuff to soak up that great gravy.

MAKES 4 TO 6 SERVINGS

For the steak:
2 cups self-rising flour
¼ cup cornstarch
2½ teaspoons seasoning salt
1 teaspoon garlic powder
1 teaspoon onion powder
½ teaspoon ground black pepper
1 egg
1½ cups buttermilk
6 cubed steaks (about 2 pounds)
2 cups vegetable oil, for deep-frying

For the sausage gravy:
½ pound ground pork sausage
2 tablespoons vegetable oil (reserved from frying)
⅓ cup all-purpose flour
2 cups whole milk
Kosher salt and black pepper, to taste

◇◇◇◇◇◇◇◇◇◇◇◇◇◇◇◇◇◇◇◇◇◇◇◇◇◇

Green onions, for garnish

◆ In a large ziplock freezer bag, combine the flour, cornstarch, seasoning salt, garlic powder, onion powder, and black pepper. Shake the bag until everything is well incorporated, then set to the side.

CONTINUED

- In a medium bowl, combine the egg and buttermilk and mix well with a whisk.

- Dip each of the cubed steaks in the buttermilk mixture, then place the steaks in the freezer bag. Shake the bag until the steaks are well coated, then remove the steaks from the bag and set them to the side.

- Pour vegetable oil into a deep fryer or deep-frying pan, and heat the oil to 350 to 360 degrees F. Deep-fry each steak for about 5 minutes, until it's golden and crispy. Remove from the fryer with tongs and place the steaks on a wire rack.

- Meanwhile, start browning the pork sausage in a large pan over medium heat, for about 5 minutes. Once the sausage is browned, remove the sausage, but leave the sausage drippings in the pan.

- Add the vegetable oil to the pan and sprinkle in the flour. Cook the flour for 2 minutes over medium heat, and be sure to whisk it so that it doesn't burn. Pour in the milk and whisk. Make sure there aren't any lumps. Once the milk gravy starts to thicken, add the sausage back into the pan, and stir.

- Sprinkle in some salt and pepper to taste, stir, and turn off the heat. Serve the chicken fried steaks with the sausage gravy on top or on the side. Garnish with green onions.

Why It's Better to Under Season Than to Over Season

Have you ever had someone's cooking, and they over seasoned?! Well, I have, and there's no way to fix that when you're sitting at the table. There have been times when I've eaten food so salty that I felt that I was going to pass out. That's why I'm super careful when it comes to seasoning, doing my best to get it just right and never to overdo it. But if you're going to season wrong, you want to under season it—if you under season a dish, people can always add some salt and pepper to it at the table. If you over season, you will be talked about! Feel free to adjust seasonings to your likings, but don't overdo it. Especially if you're serving it to others.

Shrimp and Crab Omelettes

If we're going out to a big important brunch in my family, we're heading to a place called Salty's in West Seattle. On top of all the brunch classics, it's a seafood restaurant, so they've got a huge spread—you can even customize your own omelette. I'm a soul food girl, but I'm also from the Pacific Northwest, and we love seafood here.

In this at-home copycat version of the omelettes I'd make there, the saltiness from the crab keeps the eggs well seasoned (I can't stand bland eggs!) and the addition of Havarti cheese is my secret to making it extra creamy—along with the heavy cream, of course.

People don't combine seafood and cheese much, but it's delicious and they should!

MAKES 1 SERVING

4 eggs	¼ cup fresh spinach
3 tablespoons heavy cream	¼ cup cooked shrimp meat
Kosher salt and black pepper, to taste	¼ cup lump crab meat
1 tablespoon olive oil	¼ cup shredded Havarti cheese
¼ cup sliced mushrooms	

◆ In a small mixing bowl, combine the eggs and heavy cream and beat until well combined. Sprinkle in the salt and pepper, and mix. Set to the side.

◆ Drizzle the olive oil into a large pan over medium heat. When the oil is hot, toss the mushrooms and spinach into the pan, and cook until tender. Remove from the pan and set to the side.

◆ Pour in the eggs and cook for 2 minutes. Sprinkle in the shrimp, crab, cheese, mushrooms, and spinach. Fold the omelette in half and cook for 2 more minutes, then remove from the pan. Serve and enjoy!

Smoked Salmon Eggs Benedict

When you've got tons of good seafood like we do in the Pacific Northwest, the usual ham and eggs can get a little boring. Seattle is salmon country: it's on menus all over the place. You can always find smoked salmon in stores, and you can make your own with the recipe on page 169.

But if we ever had any leftover smoked salmon when I was growing up, my mom would use it to make us a fancy little brunch. She would toil over her hollandaise sauce, stirring it and watching it until it came together just right. I spent too many mornings sitting there, watching impatiently. When I want some eggs Benedict, I want it quickly! I adapted this easy blender recipe for hollandaise from Serious Eats and haven't looked back: it's just as good and takes only about three minutes to make. The most important step is that you need the melted butter to be good and hot, or it won't cook the egg yolk.

MAKES 8 SERVINGS

4 English muffins, split
1 pound smoked salmon (page 169)
8 eggs, poached
Chopped fresh parsley
Coarse black pepper

For the hollandaise sauce:
1 egg yolk
1 teaspoon fresh lemon juice
1 tablespoon water
1 cup (2 sticks) salted butter, melted
2 dashes Tabasco sauce
½ teaspoon ground white pepper
1 teaspoon kosher salt

◆ Place the English muffins on individual plates, then top each of them with a ¼ pound smoked salmon and a poached egg. Set to the side.

◆ Add all of the ingredients for the hollandaise sauce into a blender, then blend the ingredients until well combined.

◆ Drizzle the hollandaise sauce all over the eggs. Sprinkle the parsley and black pepper on top, serve, and enjoy!

Pan-Fried Pork Chops

◇◇

Pork chops are a staple of the soul food kitchen, but while the deep-fried thick-cut pork chops that my aunt Frances first taught me to make are dinner food, these thin-cut, lightly fried ones are 100 percent a breakfast food. They go with grits, eggs, maybe even some pancakes, depending on how you're feeling—much like you would have bacon or sausage on your plate.

For these, you want to make sure you have thin-cut bone-in chops, because the bone helps keep a lot of that flavor in the meat while it's cooking, and the thinness means they're quick to cook and keeps them light enough for breakfast—a little goes a long way!

MAKES 4 TO 6 SERVINGS

4 to 6 thin-cut bone-in pork chops
   (about 1½ pounds)
2 tablespoons all-purpose flour
2 teaspoons seasoning salt
1 teaspoon onion powder

½ teaspoon ground black pepper
½ teaspoon paprika
¼ teaspoon cayenne pepper
¼ cup vegetable oil

◆ Place the pork chops on a baking sheet, then set to the side.

◆ In a small bowl, combine the flour, salt, onion powder, black pepper, paprika, and cayenne. Mix well. Sprinkle the seasoned flour all over the pork chops. Be sure to get both sides.

◆ Pour the vegetable oil into a large skillet over medium-high heat. Once the oil is hot, add the pork chops and fry each side for 5 to 7 minutes, or until golden brown. Remove from the pan, serve, and enjoy!

Creamy Cheesy Grits

<><><><><><><><><><><><><><><><><><><><><><><><><><><><><><><><><>

We had grits almost every single day when I was a kid, but cheesy grits were a special meal, reserved only for weekends. That's one of the best parts about being an adult: I can have cheesy grits anytime I want.

Even though they're made with something called "quick grits," I've got bad news for anyone looking for a shortcut: the secret to creamy grits is nothing groundbreaking, just time and plenty of patience. Low heat, a bit of heavy cream, and just waiting until the grits themselves decide to come together and thicken up. But if, after that, you want the secret to making them extra creamy, I've got something you might not have thought of: my favorite Havarti cheese. I still add the classic cheddar too, along with some salted butter, because that provides the traditional flavor. I like pairing these grits with eggs and my Pan-Fried Pork Chops (page 47).

MAKES 4 TO 6 SERVINGS	
3 cups water	½ teaspoon ground black pepper
½ cup heavy cream	½ cup shredded creamy Havarti
1 cup quick grits	cheese
4 tablespoons salted butter	½ cup shredded sharp cheddar
1 teaspoon kosher salt	cheese

◆ In a medium saucepan over high heat, pour in the water and heavy cream. Once it reaches a full boil, sprinkle in the grits and whisk. Reduce the heat to medium low and cook for 30 to 35 minutes, stirring occasionally to prevent lumps.

◆ Add the butter, and sprinkle in the salt, pepper, and cheese. Stir until everything is nice and creamy and well combined. Turn the heat off, then serve with your favorite breakfast dishes.

Everybody's Favorite Snacks

Shrimp Sliders

Crab cakes are the classic, but I'm more of a shrimp girl, so I switched out the shellfish and made my own version—and it might be even better. See, the texture of shrimp is just halfway between the crab cake and a burger, so when I made this for a little football get-together, I discovered that they fit right into a slider bun for easy eating.

By grinding most of the shrimp in the food processor and hand-chopping the remaining shrimp, the patty keeps its shape, but you still get the big chunks of shrimp for texture. When I serve them, I fry the patties up nice and golden and set them on the buns, then put out a tray of toppings for everyone to build their own sandwich with sliced onions, avocados, tomatoes, and mayonnaise.

MAKES 12 SERVINGS

1½ pounds jumbo raw shrimp, peeled and deveined, divided

¼ cup chopped green onion

1 teaspoon minced garlic

1½ teaspoons Creole seasoning

½ teaspoon ground black pepper

2 eggs, lightly beaten

½ cup all-purpose flour

½ cup vegetable oil, for frying

12 slider buns

◆ Toss about three-quarters of the shrimp into a blender or food processor, and pulse until the shrimp is well ground. Place the ground shrimp into a large mixing bowl.

◆ Chop the remaining shrimp into small pieces, and toss it into the bowl with the ground shrimp. Add in the green onion, garlic, Creole seasoning, and black pepper. Mix well.

◆ Pour in the beaten eggs and use your hands or a kitchen utensil to mix. Sprinkle in the flour and mix until it's well incorporated.

◆ Form 12 patties from the shrimp mixture and set to the side.

◆ Drizzle vegetable oil into a large skillet over medium heat. Once the oil is hot, start adding in the shrimp, 3 to 4 patties at a time. Cook each side for 5 minutes until golden brown.

◆ Place the shrimp patties on the slider buns, and let guests add their desired toppings.

Creole Pork and Shrimp Egg Rolls

◇◇

Living in Seattle, we have so many great kinds of food, and I do love ordering in crunchy egg rolls and hot Filipino lumpia. But when I make this kind of food myself, I can't help but let my Creole tastes drive the flavor. And by now you know what that means: shrimp, pork, and lots and lots of Creole seasoning. Once I fry them up, I set them out with Mae Ploy sweet chili sauce.

MAKES 12 SERVINGS

½ pound ground pork

¼ cup chopped red onions

2 tablespoons diced green bell peppers

1 teaspoon minced garlic

2½ teaspoons Creole seasoning

½ pound medium raw shrimp, peeled, deveined, and roughly chopped

1 package of egg roll wrappers

1 egg, beaten, for sealing rolls

2 cups vegetable oil, for deep-frying

◆ In a large pan over medium heat, brown the ground pork. Once browned, drain the fat from the pan into a jar and discard.

◆ Add the onions, peppers, garlic, and Creole seasoning. Cook until the onions and peppers are tender, then add the shrimp and cook for 2 more minutes. Turn off the heat.

◆ Place the egg roll wrappers on a flat surface, add the filling on top, then roll. Brush egg on the seams to help seal the rolls.

◆ Pour vegetable oil into a deep fryer or deep-frying pan. Deep-fry the egg rolls until they are nice and golden.

◆ Let cool on a wire rack, then serve with your favorite dipping sauce.

Fried Lemon Pepper Wings

FAN FAVE!

Lemon pepper chicken wings are a staple of Atlanta food, but I am not from Atlanta and I didn't grow up on those, so I just want to warn you, these are nothing like those ones. These are my own zesty, crispy creation, and they will rock your next football party. The light battering and heavy seasoning doubles up on the crunch and fills the wings with bright pops of flavor. I like to set them out on a tray with fresh lemon wedges so that people can squeeze on a little extra before they eat them. They also go well with my blue cheese dressing (page 70).

MAKES 4 SERVINGS

¼ cup lemon juice

2 pounds chicken wings

2 teaspoons garlic powder, divided

2 teaspoons onion powder, divided

1 teaspoon Old Bay Seasoning

1½ cups all-purpose flour

2 teaspoons lemon pepper

1 teaspoon dried parsley flakes (optional)

2 cups vegetable oil, for deep-frying

◆ In a large mixing bowl, pour the lemon juice over the chicken, then season the chicken with 1 teaspoon of the garlic powder, 1 teaspoon of the onion powder, and the Old Bay Seasoning. Use your hands to toss the chicken and make sure it is well coated with the seasonings.

◆ In a medium-size bowl, add the flour, the remaining 1 teaspoon garlic powder and 1 teaspoon onion powder, lemon pepper, and parsley flakes. Use your hands or a utensil to make sure the seasonings are well distributed throughout the flour. Coat the chicken wings with the seasoned flour, and set aside on a plate.

◆ In your deep fryer or pan, pour in the oil. Heat the oil to 350 to 360 degrees F. Place the chicken into the hot oil and fry until it's golden. To ensure it's done, pierce the chicken down to the bone with a small knife or fork. If no blood is visible, the chicken is done.

◆ Place the chicken on a paper-towel-lined baking sheet or plate for 2 minutes to cool slightly. Serve with lemon wedges or your favorite dipping sauces.

Spicy Corn Dip

This is my dream dip: it's creamy, chunky, spicy, and filled with things I always have on hand. I actually came up with it when my husband called me to say that the cable was out at his friend's house, and he and all his friends were going to come watch the football game at our house. You know I can't have people over without serving them something delicious, so I just started cooking with what was on hand, adding in ingredients until it tasted just right, then serving it all up with a bag of tortilla chips. The result was almost too good—they wanted to come watch at our house every week, and they wanted that dip to be there! I had to write down what I'd done before I forgot so I could make it again.

MAKES 6 SERVINGS

1 tablespoon extra-virgin olive oil

½ pound spicy Italian sausage

1 medium red onion, diced

1 large red bell pepper, diced

1 cup sour cream

4 ounces cream cheese, at room temperature

4 cups frozen corn, thawed

½ cup chopped green onions

1 large jalapeño, diced

4 garlic cloves, chopped

1 tablespoon chopped cilantro

2 teaspoons Creole seasoning

1 teaspoon ground black pepper

1 cup shredded sharp cheddar cheese, divided

1 cup shredded Colby Jack cheese, divided

Vegetable oil, for greasing

◆ Preheat the oven to 350 degrees F.

◆ In a large pan over medium heat, heat the oil. Add the Italian sausage, and cook until it browns. Toss in the onions and bell peppers. Cook until they soften.

◆ Add the sour cream and cream cheese. Stir until well combined, then add the corn, green onion, jalapeño, garlic, and cilantro. Continue to stir the ingredients until everything is well incorporated. Sprinkle in the Creole seasoning, black pepper, ½ cup of the cheddar, and ½ cup of the Colby Jack cheese. Mix well.

◆ Lightly grease a baking dish, then add in the corn mixture. Top with the remaining cheese and bake, uncovered, for 20 minutes. Cool slightly before serving.

Crab Deviled Eggs with Bacon

◇◇

If you read the breakfast section, you know I hate bland eggs. So when I wanted to make some deviled eggs for a holiday party, I knew I needed to add my special twist. Crab packs the filling with briny flavor, and the bacon adds a smoky, meaty crunch. Because I was using the crab, I figured I should throw in some Old Bay, the seafood spice that's basically crab's best friend.

Here in Seattle, it's easy to pick up lump crab meat from my local seafood market, but if that isn't an option where you live, you can substitute canned crab. Whichever way you go, though, make sure to pick through the crab to double-check that there are no shell fragments—nothing's worse than biting into a crab shell!

MAKES 14 SERVINGS

7 hard-boiled eggs

⅓ cup mayonnaise

1 teaspoon yellow mustard

6 ounces cooked lump crab meat, plus more for garnish

1 tablespoon dill relish

1 tablespoon minced onion

1 teaspoon minced garlic

1½ teaspoons Old Bay Seasoning

5 slices cooked bacon, chopped

Chopped fresh parsley (optional)

◆ Peel the eggs, then cut the eggs lengthwise. Scoop out the yolks and place them into a medium mixing bowl. Mash the yolks using a fork until they are nice and creamy. Add the mayonnaise and mustard, and mix until well combined. Set to the side.

◆ Carefully pick through the lump crab meat to make sure that there aren't any shells. Then add the crab meat into the yolk mixture, followed by the relish, onion, garlic, and Old Bay Seasoning. Mix the ingredients.

◆ Stuff the eggs with the mixture, then top with the sliced bacon and the parsley. Garnish with extra crab.

Buffalo Turkey Wings with Blue Cheese Dressing

◇◇

My husband loves my cooking, but his number one complaint is that there's never enough. We were digging into my chicken wings one day and they were great, but he said there just wasn't enough meat. I decided right then, the next time I made wings, I was going to go Flintstone-style for him.

Chicken wings are usually a little over an ounce of meat each, and turkey wings have about three ounces of meat on them. That means you get the same crispy skin and spicy buffalo flavor, along with the added richness of the built-in turkey flavor, but way more meat. It started as a joke about cooking something big enough for him, and now it's what he always wants. You just need to remember that it takes a little more time to cook them than the standard chicken version. Serve these with celery sticks and plenty of my blue cheese dressing (page 70). Note: Sometimes turkey wings can be hard to find. Be sure to go to the meat department of your grocery store and ask them if they have any in the back. If you have no luck there, check out some of your local butchers.

MAKES 4 SERVINGS

Vegetable oil, for greasing
1 tablespoon seasoning salt
1 tablespoon garlic powder
1 tablespoon onion powder
1 tablespoon paprika
1½ teaspoons ground black pepper
1 teaspoon celery salt

2 pounds turkey wings, flats and
   drums separated
3 tablespoons olive oil
¼ cup salted butter, melted
½ cup hot sauce
Blue cheese dressing (page 70)

♦ Preheat the oven to 325 degrees F, and lightly grease a 9-by-13-inch baking dish.

♦ In a small bowl, combine the seasoning salt, garlic powder, onion powder, paprika, black pepper, and celery salt. Mix well, then set to the side.

♦ Place the turkey wings in the baking dish and drizzle them with olive oil. Rub the oil all over the wings to ensure that they are well coated. Sprinkle the seasoning mixture all over the front and back of the wings.

- Cover the baking dish with aluminum foil, and bake for 1 hour and 35 minutes. Then remove from the oven, baste the wings with the oven drippings, and set to the side.

- Combine the melted butter and hot sauce. Mix well, then pour all over the wings. Place the wings back in the oven, uncovered, and bake for another 1 hour and 30 minutes.

- Remove from the oven. Serve with the blue cheese dressing for guests to use as a dip.

Loaded Baked Potato Dip

◇◇

I love a good baked potato, loading it up with bacon, cheese, onions, and sour cream, letting all the textures and saltiness melt into a fluffy base, and then dipping my potato chips into it. *Wait! What?* I know, people think it's a bit weird, but I think it's delicious. Still, I have figured out a way to make my strange eating quirk into a socially acceptable double-potato extravaganza by turning the baked potatoes into a dip—with all the same toppings. Then I just serve it with potato chips, and suddenly people stop making fun of me and start digging in.

MAKES 8 TO 10 SERVINGS

7 jumbo baking potatoes	8 slices thick-cut bacon, cooked and crumbled, divided
1½ cups sour cream	½ cup chopped green onions, divided
½ cup (1 stick) salted butter, softened	2 teaspoons garlic powder
4 ounces cream cheese	2 teaspoons kosher salt
2 cups shredded cheddar cheese, divided	1 teaspoon ground black pepper
	Vegetable oil, for greasing

◆ Preheat the oven to 375 degrees F. While the oven is heating up, wash and scrub the potatoes under cool water.

◆ Place the potatoes in a casserole dish and bake for about 65 minutes, then remove from the oven. Let the potatoes cool. Reduce the oven temperature to 350 degrees F.

◆ In a large mixing bowl, start scooping out the meat of the potatoes. Add the sour cream, butter, and cream cheese, and mix until well incorporated. Sprinkle in 1 cup of the shredded cheese, half of the crumbled bacon, and all but 1 tablespoon of the green onions. Stir to combine, then add the garlic powder, salt, and pepper. Mix the ingredients.

◆ Lightly oil a 9-by-13-inch baking dish. Add the potato mixture and smooth it out. Sprinkle the remaining cheese, remaining bacon, and remaining green onions on top of the dip.

◆ Bake in the oven, uncovered, for 30 minutes. Serve with your favorite chips.

Fried Pickles

When I was a kid, I'd happily eat regular pickles. Then one time we were down South for a family reunion, and somebody served me fried pickles. Well, I tell you what: I never went back. My mom would serve me the same pickles I liked a few weeks earlier, and I was like, "No way!" I wanted only the fried ones.

For this recipe, the mix of the cornmeal and self-rising flour will get you a nice, light, but sturdy crunch. You want to make sure you pat the pickle chips as dry as possible so that the eggs will stick to them. Then the flour will stick to the eggs, and you won't have pickle slices slipping out of their shells all over the place. But beware, once you go fried, you might never go back!

MAKES 4 SERVINGS

1 (16–ounce) jar of dill pickle chips, drained	½ teaspoon ground black pepper
1 cup yellow cornmeal	½ teaspoon paprika
1 cup self-rising flour	½ teaspoon cayenne pepper
1 teaspoon seasoning salt	2 eggs, beaten
	¾ cup vegetable oil, for frying

♦ Pat the pickle chips dry, then place them on a paper-towel-lined baking sheet.

♦ In a large bowl, combine the cornmeal, flour, seasoning salt, black pepper, paprika, and cayenne. Mix until well combined.

♦ Coat the pickle chips with the eggs by dipping them in. Be sure to shake any excess off. Then toss the pickle chips into the flour mixture, and make sure they are well coated. Shake off the excess flour and place the chips back on the baking sheet.

♦ In a large frying pan, warm the vegetable oil to about 350 degrees F. Add the pickle chips and be sure not to overcrowd the pan. Fry the chips until they are nice and golden, 2 to 3 minutes.

♦ Remove the chips from the oil with a slotted spoon, and let cool on a wire rack. Serve with your favorite dipping sauce.

Comfort Staples: Soups, Salads, and Sandwiches

Grilled Shrimp Po'boys

There's nowhere in Seattle that serves up a po'boy that meets the standards of my Louisiana background, so I had to make my own. It's a quintessential sandwich from New Orleans, invented by a restaurant trying to support the "poor boys"—striking streetcar workers. It's made on soft bread and packed full of flavor from the Creole mayonnaise. Back in Baton Rouge, you'll mostly see fried shrimp in po'boys, but I like the flavor from the char on the grilled version. But you can also make this using the Deep-Fried Catfish on page 171.

MAKES 3 TO 4 SERVINGS

1½ pounds large raw shrimp, peeled, deveined, and tails removed
2 tablespoons extra-virgin olive oil
2½ teaspoons blackening seasoning
1 teaspoon Creole seasoning
1 teaspoon minced garlic
Vegetable oil, for the grill pan

For the Creole mayonnaise:
1 cup mayonnaise
1 tablespoon minced yellow onion
2 teaspoons honey Dijon mustard
1½ teaspoons minced garlic
1½ teaspoons Creole seasoning

3 to 4 hoagie or French rolls
2 medium tomatoes, sliced
1 cup shredded lettuce

◆ In a large mixing bowl, drizzle the shrimp with olive oil. Sprinkle in the blackening seasoning, Creole seasoning, and garlic. Toss the shrimp to mix, then set to the side.

◆ Lightly oil a grill pan and place it over medium-high heat. Once the pan is hot, add the shrimp and cook for 5 to 7 minutes. Remove the shrimp from the pan, and place on a clean plate.

◆ In a medium bowl, add the mayonnaise, onion, mustard, garlic, and Creole seasoning. Mix well.

◆ Slather your desired amount of the Creole mayonnaise on both sides of the rolls. Add the tomatoes on the bottom of the hoagie, and place the shrimp on top. Top the shrimp with shredded lettuce, serve, and enjoy!

Grilled Chicken Cobb Salad

Even though Cobb salad comes from the West Coast, it feels like something that has a little soul in it—it's got bold flavors, big crunch, and most importantly to me, plenty of bacon and cheese. I like to cook the chicken up in my grill pan because it puts those thick char marks on it. Then I pile it all into a bowl with the juicy tomatoes, tender avocados, and crisp romaine. It's one of the few salads that's hearty enough to be an entire meal.

MAKES 6 SERVINGS

For the blue cheese dressing:
1 cup mayonnaise
½ cup buttermilk
½ cup sour cream
½ cup blue cheese crumbles
1 teaspoon Tabasco sauce
¼ teaspoon coarse black pepper

1 teaspoon paprika
1 teaspoon garlic powder
½ teaspoon kosher salt

½ teaspoon ground black pepper
½ teaspoon cayenne pepper
1 pound thin-cut chicken breast
2 tablespoons vegetable oil
4 romaine hearts, chopped
2 roma tomatoes, chopped
¼ cup chopped green onions
6 slices cooked bacon, chopped
3 hard-boiled eggs, sliced
1 jumbo avocado, peeled and sliced
½ cup croutons

- In a medium bowl, combine the mayonnaise, buttermilk, and sour cream. Stir until it's nice and smooth. Then add the blue cheese crumbles, Tabasco, and black pepper. Mix until well combined and refrigerate the blue cheese dressing for a minimum of 2 hours.

- In a small bowl, combine the paprika, garlic powder, salt, black pepper, and cayenne pepper.

- Set the chicken on a plate and sprinkle the seasoning mix all over. Set to the side.

- In a medium-size grill pan over medium heat, drizzle in the oil. Once the oil is nice and hot, add the chicken and cook the breasts on each side for 8 minutes. Remove from the pan and thinly slice the chicken breast.

- In a large bowl, add the romaine lettuce, then top with tomatoes, green onions, bacon, eggs, and avocado. Toss in the croutons and chicken. Serve with the blue cheese dressing.

Pimento Cheese and Fried Green Tomato Sandwich

Pimento cheese and fried green tomatoes are two staples of Southern cuisine, so combining them into one dish will give any party a real back-home feel. It's a great one to make for a crowd because it makes a lot all at once. You'll want to start by making the cheese spread, as it has to be refrigerated for several hours. The only real work involved is frying the tomatoes, because all the flavor in the sandwich comes from the spread, and all the texture from the tomatoes themselves. Once you've got the spread and the tomatoes, you just put it together and slice it up into as many individual sandwiches as you want—you can do little two-inch ones for a finger-food party or bigger ones for a sit-down lunch.

MAKES 8 TO 12 SERVINGS

For the cheese spread:
½ cup mayonnaise
4 ounces cream cheese
3 cups shredded sharp
   cheddar cheese
1 (4-ounce) jar of diced pimentos,
   drained
1 tablespoon minced yellow onion
1 teaspoon minced garlic
1 teaspoon Worcestershire sauce
½ teaspoon ground black pepper

For the tomatoes:
1 cup self-rising flour
1 cup yellow cornmeal
½ teaspoon kosher salt
½ teaspoon ground black pepper
2 eggs
½ cup buttermilk
4 large green tomatoes, sliced
   ½ inch thick
2 cups vegetable oil, for deep-frying

2 loaves French bread, sliced in half
   lengthwise

◆ In a large bowl, combine the mayonnaise and cream cheese, and mix until well combined. Add the cheddar cheese, pimentos, onion, garlic, Worcestershire sauce, and black pepper. Mix until well incorporated, cover the bowl, and refrigerate for a minimum of 6 hours.

CONTINUED

- In a medium mixing bowl, combine the self-rising flour, cornmeal, salt, and black pepper. Mix until well incorporated and set aside.

- In another medium mixing bowl, combine the eggs and buttermilk, and mix well.

- Pat the sliced tomatoes dry with paper towels. Dip the tomatoes into the egg mixture, then into the flour mixture. Let the tomatoes sit for 5 minutes.

- In a large skillet over medium heat, pour the vegetable oil until it's 2 to 3 inches deep. Add the tomatoes and deep-fry until nice and golden, 3 to 4 minutes.

- Slather the pimento cheese on the bottom half of the French bread, then top off with the fried tomatoes and the top half of the French bread. Cut into individual sandwiches and serve.

Deep-Frying

Lots of people are scared of deep-frying, they tell me. But don't be scared of a little hot oil, just make sure you're doing it right so that it's worth the effort. The biggest mistake people make when frying food is using the wrong oil. It's important to use a high smoke-point oil when frying, or it will start to stink and ruin your food. There are many high smoke-point oils, but some of the most popular ones are peanut, canola oil, and my personal favorite, corn oil. Be sure when picking out an oil that you carefully read the ingredients on the back of the bottle, because some brands will mix high smoke-point oils with other oils that may not be of as good quality. I like the Mazola brand corn oil, and that's what I use in my frying.

Crab and Lobster Grilled Cheese

I owe an apology for this recipe. See, it was something one of my fans requested quite a while ago. She'd seen a version on Pinterest and knew that cheese and seafood was just my style and I could make an even better one. And I did! But it was just so good that I had to hold on to it for this book. I kept it for myself, right up until now. I'm sorry, but also, you will understand once you put together this seafood-and-cheese lover's dream.

MAKES 2 SERVINGS	
½ cup cooked lobster meat	½ teaspoon minced garlic
½ cup cooked crab meat	4 slices Texas toast garlic bread
2 tablespoons salted butter, melted	4 thick slices sharp cheddar cheese
1 teaspoon Old Bay Seasoning	4 thick slices Havarti cheese

◆ In a large mixing bowl, toss the lobster, crab, melted butter, Old Bay Seasoning, and garlic. Mix well, then set the bowl to the side.

◆ Lay two slices of Texas toast on a plate, and top each with a slice of cheddar and Havarti. Divide the seafood mixture in half and add half to each slice of toast. Top the seafood with the remaining cheese and bread slices.

◆ Use a sandwich press or hot skillet to grill each side of the sandwich until it is golden brown and the cheese is melted. Serve and enjoy!

Clam, Shrimp, and Crab Chowder

I'm not much of a soup person, much to my mom's dismay—she would make it all the time when I was a kid, and I got very tired of it. But if you make a nice, thick chowder and jam it full of all my favorite Northwest seafoods—shrimp, clams, and crab—along with a healthy helping of onions, garlic, celery, and potatoes, it's not a soup anymore, it's pure comfort in a bowl. I like it thick and rich enough that I can sprinkle it with crackers and drag big pieces of crusty bread through as I eat it.

MAKES 10 SERVINGS

½ pound bacon, chopped
1 large yellow onion, diced
2 medium carrots, peeled and diced
2 stalks celery, diced
2½ cups seafood stock
2 large red potatoes, peeled and diced
3 garlic cloves, minced
¾ cup (1½ sticks) salted butter
¾ cup all-purpose flour

2 cups heavy cream
2 cups whole milk
1 cup minced clams
½ cup crab meat
2 teaspoons kosher salt
1 teaspoon ground black pepper
½ pound medium raw shrimp, peeled and deveined
2 tablespoons chopped fresh parsley

◆ Toss the bacon into a large stockpot, and turn the heat to medium. Cook the bacon until it is crisp. Then remove it from the pot, reserving the fat in the pot, and set the bacon to the side.

◆ Add the onion, carrot, and celery to the pot. Cook until they are nice and tender, then pour in the seafood stock. Add the potatoes and garlic, and simmer for about 15 minutes, still on medium heat.

◆ While that's cooking, in a medium saucepan, add the butter and melt it over medium heat. Sprinkle in the flour and whisk. Cook for 3 minutes, stirring continuously, then pour in the cream and milk. Be sure to whisk so it's lump-free!

◆ Pour the butter-and-flour mixture into the large pot with the other ingredients, and stir. Add the clams, crab, salt, and black pepper. Mix the ingredients, then reduce the heat to low.

◆ Add the shrimp and bacon, and stir. Simmer for 15 minutes. Top off with fresh parsley before serving.

Brunswick Stew

<><><><><><><><><><><><><><><><><><><><><><><><><><><><><><><><><><>

Every time that I make my Brunswick Stew, my North Carolina friends say I make it North Carolina style, and my Georgia friends say it's *their* style. What's the difference? I'm not really sure—some people use pork, some use chicken, some, like me, use both. All I know is this is how I make mine because it's how my mom made hers, and we use these meats because we're mostly just trying to use up whatever was left over from a barbecue. Let's just call it Rosie style and sit down to share a big ol' bowl of soul.

MAKES 8 TO 10 SERVINGS

6 cups chicken broth

2 cups Slow Cooker BBQ Pulled Pork (page 142)

2 cups chopped chicken, cooked

2 cups frozen or dry lima beans (if dry, soak overnight prior)

3 medium russet potatoes, peeled and diced

1 (14-ounce) can diced tomatoes in tomato juice

1 large red onion, diced

1½ cups frozen peas and carrots

1½ cups frozen okra

1 cup frozen corn

1 cup hickory BBQ sauce

3 garlic cloves, minced

2 tablespoons Worcestershire sauce

2½ teaspoons seasoning salt

1 teaspoon ground black pepper

½ teaspoon ground cumin

◆ Add all of the ingredients to a 6-quart slow cooker. Stir until everything is well incorporated. Put the lid on the slow cooker, and set the heat on low.

◆ Cook for 5 hours, then serve. Any leftovers can be stored in an airtight container in the refrigerator for up to 5 days.

Crab Salad Cups

Pop quiz: Guests are coming over, and you've got to get something quick, easy, and delicious on the table soon so that they can eat and you guys can get on with the business of catching up. What do you do? The answer: crab salad cups.

These were requested by a subscriber who was looking for something a little more healthful to put out for guests, and once I made them, I knew they'd be a staple for me too. Whenever I'm hosting a gathering and pushing for time, I always make these. They are crowd-pleasers (and if you have a crowd, it's easy to double or triple the recipe) and take less than 10 minutes to whip up. If you don't want to spend a little extra money on real crab, feel free to use imitation crab meat!

MAKES 4 SERVINGS

1 pound cooked crab meat, real or imitation	1 small red bell pepper, diced
½ cup mayonnaise	1 garlic clove, minced
2 stalks celery, diced	1 teaspoon Old Bay Seasoning
1 small red onion, diced	4 small romaine lettuce leaves
	2 tablespoons chopped fresh parsley

◆ In a large mixing bowl, add the crab, mayonnaise, celery, onion, pepper, garlic, and Old Bay Seasoning. Stir the ingredients.

◆ Scoop the salad mix into the romaine lettuce leaves, and top off with chopped parsley before serving.

Seven-Layer Shrimp Louie Salad

The best way to get me to eat a salad is to layer it—somehow being able to crunch through the beautiful stacks of ingredients is just more appealing to me. Maybe because it reminds me of one of my favorite foods, lasagna! This layered salad takes the classic Shrimp Louie and makes it into a rainbow stunner, with the bright green of the lettuce and avocado, the pink of the shrimp and Thousand Island dressing, the purple of the onions, the red of the tomatoes, and the white and yellow of the eggs. It's simple, gorgeous, stacked with textures and colors, and will fill you right up.

MAKES 10 TO 12 SERVINGS

3 romaine lettuce hearts, chopped	3 large avocados, peeled and sliced
1 large red onion, diced	3 pounds cooked small shrimp
6 hard-boiled eggs, peeled and sliced	2 cups croutons
6 small roma tomatoes, chopped	Thousand Island salad dressing

---

◆ In a large bowl, add the lettuce. Next add a layer of onion. Then add a layer of egg, a layer of tomato, a layer of avocado, and a layer of shrimp. Over the top, add a layer of croutons. Serve and enjoy with Thousand Island or your favorite salad dressing.

Black-Eyed Pea Salad

<><><><><><><><><><><><><><><><><><><><><><><><><><><><><><><><>

Every New Year's Day when I was a kid, we would eat black-eyed peas because beans mean prosperity, and we were always hoping that this would be the year. In fact, we hoped so hard we would put out two kinds of black-eyed peas: the traditional hot version, made with ham hocks, and also this nice cold salad—why not double your luck? As kids, we loved this version for all of the great colors. Now I love serving it with my Sweet Cornbread (page 122) and crumbling a little bit of it right on top.

MAKES 6 TO 8 SERVINGS

2 (14.5–ounce) cans black-eyed peas, drained	½ medium red onion, diced
8 slices cooked bacon, chopped	2 tablespoons extra-virgin olive oil
2 large roma tomatoes, chopped	2 teaspoons hot sauce
1 medium green bell pepper, diced	½ teaspoon ground black pepper
	4 romaine hearts, chopped

◆ In a large bowl, combine the black-eyed peas, bacon, tomatoes, bell pepper, and onion.

◆ In a small bowl, combine the olive oil, hot sauce, and black pepper. Mix well using a whisk.

◆ Drizzle the olive oil mixture all over the black-eyed peas. Toss in the romaine, then mix the ingredients. Serve with your favorite dressing.

Side Dishes for Supper Time

Green Beans, Potatoes, and Bacon

FAN FAVE!

◇◇

This was a pretty typical dish for us growing up, so I was surprised when I posted this on Facebook and it got over a million views in the first week. It's one of the videos that helped my Facebook page take off, and I love that I get to share a staple from my house with so many other people. It's cheap, easy, and delicious, and because it has the meat, vegetable, and starch all right in the same pot, it's basically a full meal all in one (though if you're greedy like me, go ahead and grab a piece of cornbread as well!).

MAKES 6 SERVINGS

1 pound bacon ends, chopped

1 pound baby red potatoes, cut in halves or quarters

1 (16-ounce) bag of frozen green beans, or 1 pound fresh-cut green beans

3 cups chicken broth

1 medium yellow onion, chopped

1 large jalapeño pepper, chopped (optional)

1½ tablespoons minced garlic

½ teaspoon cracked black pepper

◆ Add all of the ingredients to a 6-quart slow cooker. Turn the slow cooker on high and cover. Cook for 4 hours, then serve.

Soul Food Macaroni and Cheese

You know how Cookie Monster feels about cookies? That's me and macaroni and cheese. My mom would wake up early every Sunday to get started on dinner. She'd turn on the radio, play that good ol' R & B (explains why I listen to R & B while I cook!), and go in. My mom would be in the kitchen all Sunday, peeling potatoes for her Southern potato salad and cleaning fresh greens that she bought from the market. I'd just observe everything and patiently wait for her to ask me to sample something. And there was nothing I liked sampling more than macaroni and cheese—I had a thousand reasons why I needed two bites to "make sure" it would come out right.

Asking me to choose a favorite macaroni and cheese recipe is like asking me to choose between Morris Chestnut and Idris Elba, though. I want it all! But when I had to pick one that deserved a spot in the book, I knew this was it. It's a special one, the one I make for holidays, in part because it uses six kinds of cheese (so it can get expensive). The cream cheese and Havarti make this super creamy and add a little tang, while the mozzarella adds stretch to it. The sharp cheddar and Colby Jack add the big flavor. You really do need them all—the result is absolutely worth it.

MAKES 12 SERVINGS

1 teaspoon kosher salt, for boiling the pasta

1 pound uncooked elbow pasta

4 tablespoons unsalted butter

2 tablespoons all-purpose flour

1½ cups half-and-half

1 cup evaporated milk

4 ounces cream cheese

8 ounces Gouda cheese, shredded or cubed

8 ounces Havarti cheese, shredded or cubed

1 teaspoon seasoning salt or plain kosher salt

1 teaspoon smoked paprika

1 teaspoon onion powder

1 teaspoon garlic powder

½ teaspoon freshly cracked black pepper

8 ounces sharp cheddar cheese, shredded

4 ounces mozzarella cheese, shredded

4 ounces Colby Jack cheese, shredded

CONTINUED

◆ Preheat the oven to 350 degrees F.

◆ In a large stockpot over high heat, pour about 2 quarts of water and sprinkle in the kosher salt. Bring the water to a boil, then add in the pasta. Cook the pasta until it is al dente (cooked but still firm), then drain the pasta and rinse it under cool water. Return the pasta to the stockpot and set to the side.

◆ Place a large saucepan over medium heat, then toss in the butter. Melt the butter down completely, then sprinkle in the flour. Whisk the ingredients until they are well incorporated, then pour in the half-and-half and evaporated milk. Whisk the ingredients and continue to cook over medium heat for about 3 minutes.

◆ Reduce the heat to low, then add in the cream cheese, Gouda, and Havarti. Stir the mixture until the cheese melts and you have a nice, creamy cheese sauce. Sprinkle in the seasoning salt, paprika, onion powder, garlic powder, and pepper. Mix until well incorporated.

◆ Pour the cheese sauce over the macaroni pasta in the stockpot. Stir everything until it is well combined, then pour half of the macaroni-and-cheese mixture into a 9-by-13-inch baking dish. Sprinkle half of the sharp cheddar, mozzarella, and Colby Jack on top of the mac and cheese. Next, add the remaining macaroni and cheese into the baking dish and top it off with the remaining cheese.

◆ Bake the macaroni and cheese for 25 to 30 minutes. Remove from the oven and let sit for 5 to 10 minutes before serving.

Cheesy Whipped Potatoes

◇◇

When I was younger, I hated potatoes—with the exception of french fries, of course! If someone made mashed or whipped potatoes, I simply would not eat them. But my mom knew how much I loved cheese, so she started adding cheese to her whipped potatoes to get me to eat them, and suddenly I fell in love—and I'm still in love with these now.

But the important part to me today is that these are whipped instead of mashed, so they don't get lumpy or gluey. To be able to whip them properly, you have to make sure you really cook the heck out of the potatoes—they should be fork-tender. Then they're ready to serve up with some Beef Meatloaf (page 155) or Southern Fried Chicken (page 158).

MAKES 8 TO 10 SERVINGS

9 to 10 medium russet potatoes, washed, peeled, and chopped

6 cups chicken broth

6 tablespoons salted butter

1 cup half-and-half

1½ cups shredded sharp cheddar cheese

2 teaspoons kosher salt

½ teaspoon ground black pepper

- In a large stockpot over high heat, add the chopped potatoes and the chicken broth. Boil until the potatoes are nice and tender, usually 15 minutes. Drain the broth from the potatoes.

- In a large bowl, whip the potatoes using a whisk or a handheld mixer until they are nice and lump-free. Add the butter and the half-and-half. Stir the ingredients until everything is well combined.

- Sprinkle in the cheese, salt, and pepper. Stir the potatoes until they are nice and creamy, then serve.

Baked Candied Yams

FAN FAVE!

If you do a Google search for candied yams, my recipe is right there at the top—where it deserves to be; it's really that good! When I was growing up, my mom would just put out canned yams, so I would always look forward to the holidays when my aunt Nisha would make the real-deal candied ones. Now that I'm making my own, I do them in the oven rather than on the stove, because when they bake up in that syrup, they come out even more tender and sweet.

MAKES 6 TO 8 SERVINGS

---

5 medium yams, washed, peeled, and
　sliced about ½ inch thick
½ cup (1 stick) salted butter
1 cup granulated sugar
¼ cup brown sugar

1 teaspoon ground cinnamon
½ teaspoon ground nutmeg
¼ teaspoon ground cloves
¼ teaspoon ground ginger
1 tablespoon vanilla extract

◆ Preheat the oven to 350 degrees F. In a 9-by-13-inch baking dish, arrange the yams.

◆ In a medium saucepan over medium heat, melt the butter. Once the butter is melted, sprinkle in the sugars, cinnamon, nutmeg, cloves, and ginger. Turn the heat off, mix the ingredients, add in the vanilla, and stir.

◆ Pour the candied mixture over the yams, and coat them thoroughly. Cover the baking dish with aluminum foil and bake for 30 minutes. Remove the yams from the oven and baste them with the candied mixture in the dish. Then cover the yams again and bake for another 15 to 20 minutes.

◆ Remove the yams from the oven and let them sit for about 10 minutes. Baste them again with the candied mixture before serving.

Southern Potato Salad

FAN FAVE!

In my family, everybody has an assigned dish for the family picnic and all the other get-togethers, and my mom's was the potato salad—I think because she made it the most like *her mom's*, and when you have seventeen brothers and sisters, that's what everybody wants.

But listen, I think I might even outdo my mom's version. She always used chopped dill pickles, but I go big and use lots of sweet and dill relish and one very special secret ingredient that makes all the difference. See, there are two things you need for a perfect potato salad. The first is texture (you want to cook those potatoes super well; nobody wants rocks in their salad), and the second is seasoning. And the key to that seasoning? Pickle juice!

MAKES 6 TO 8 SERVINGS

4 large russet potatoes, peeled and chopped	1 teaspoon garlic powder
3 hard-boiled eggs, peeled	½ cup mayonnaise
¼ cup diced celery	¼ cup sweet relish
¼ cup chopped green onion	⅓ cup dill relish
1½ teaspoons onion powder	2 tablespoons yellow mustard
1 teaspoon cracked black pepper	2 tablespoons dill pickle juice
1 teaspoon kosher salt	Paprika (optional)

◆ In a large pot over high heat, boil the potatoes until they are nice and tender, 10 to 15 minutes. Once done, drain the water and let the potatoes cool before transferring to a large bowl.

◆ Crumble the eggs into the bowl with the potatoes. Add the celery and onion, and stir. Sprinkle in the onion powder, black pepper, salt, and garlic powder. Mix well, then set the bowl to the side.

◆ In a small bowl, combine the mayonnaise, relishes, mustard, and pickle juice. Mix well, then add to the potatoes. Fold all of the ingredients until they are well combined, cover, and refrigerate until the potato salad is nice and cold. Serve with paprika sprinkled on top.

Seafood Macaroni Salad

Back when I was a kid, there was a restaurant in our area called King's Table, a buffet where you could eat as much as you wanted for seven dollars—fried fish, mashed potatoes, roast beef, three chocolate sundaes, you name it. But even as a kid, I went straight for the seafood, specifically the seafood pasta salad. I liked it so much that my mom even played around in the kitchen to try to make it for me. I liked hers, but in my version, I did one little thing that made it even better: I added even more seafood. What makes this so great is how the macaroni wraps around the chunks of shrimp and crab, so you want to make sure there's enough seafood to get some in every bite!

MAKES 10 SERVINGS

1 teaspoon kosher salt, for boiling the pasta	1 teaspoon Old Bay Seasoning
3 cups dry elbow pasta (large or small will work)	1 teaspoon minced garlic
	1 pound cooked shrimp, peeled
1 cup mayonnaise	1 pound imitation crab meat
¼ cup lemon juice	¼ cup chopped green onion
2 tablespoons yellow mustard	⅓ cup diced celery
1 teaspoon Cajun seasoning	½ cup sliced black olives
	1 tablespoon dried parsley flakes

◆ In a medium pot over high heat, bring water and salt to a boil. Add the pasta and cook until it's al dente. Drain the pasta once done, and rinse it under cold water to stop the cooking process.

◆ In a large bowl, combine the mayonnaise, lemon juice, and mustard. Mix until well combined. Then sprinkle in the Cajun seasoning, Old Bay Seasoning, and garlic. Mix well.

◆ Add the seafood and toss or stir in the bowl until it's covered with the dressing. Add the onions, celery, olives, and pasta. Fold all of the ingredients, sprinkle in the dried parsley flakes, and fold again. Cover the pasta and refrigerate for at least 1 hour before serving.

Coleslaw

<><><><><><><><><><><><><><><><><><><><><><><><><><><><><><><>

Lean in, cousins, I've got a secret for you. I rarely whisper, but I can't be shouting this out loud: I don't love coleslaw. I know, I know, I should love it. But I don't, and that's okay—I still make sure that I know how to cook the very best version for all the wonderful people in my life who *do* love coleslaw. They've helped me to figure out that the most important thing is to just keep it simple and give it plenty of time to rest in the fridge so that the flavors come together. And, to be clear, I'm not against putting it into a sandwich with my Slow Cooker BBQ Pulled Pork (page 142).

MAKES 8 TO 10 SERVINGS

2 cups mayonnaise

¼ cup granulated sugar (optional, if
   you want it sweet)

2 teaspoons yellow mustard

2 teaspoons kosher salt

½ teaspoon ground black pepper

1 large head of green cabbage,
   shredded

2 large carrots, peeled and shredded

◆ In a large bowl, combine the mayonnaise, sugar, mustard, salt, and pepper. Mix until well combined, then add the shredded cabbage and carrots. Toss until well coated. Cover the bowl and refrigerate for at least 1 hour, or until cold, before serving.

Soul Food Collard Greens

Collard greens were a staple in my home while growing up—we could never have a holiday without them; we could barely eat a dinner without them. But while Mom usually made her collard greens with ham hocks, I like to make mine with bacon ends. They're about the same price, but they cook a little quicker than the ham hocks and give the dish a nice smoky flavor. Let's face it—bacon drippings make everything taste better! When you serve them up, you'll want to make sure you have Sweet Cornbread (page 122) on the table so everyone can sop up the pot likker—that smoky, savory liquid left behind from cooking the greens.

MAKES 6 SERVINGS

1 pound bacon ends, chopped, plus more for garnish	4 pounds collard greens, cleaned and cut (see page 101)
1 large yellow onion, diced	1 teaspoon seasoning salt
1 teaspoon minced garlic	½ teaspoon ground black pepper
6 cups chicken broth	1 large jalapeño pepper, sliced
2 cups water	2 to 3 tablespoons distilled white vinegar

◆ In a stockpot over medium heat, brown the bacon.

◆ Once the bacon is browned, add the onions and cook until the onions start to sweat, 3 to 5 minutes. Add the garlic and cook for 1 more minute.

◆ Pour in the chicken broth, turn the heat up to high, and boil for 20 minutes.

◆ Pour in the water and turn the heat down to medium. Start adding the collard greens into the pot. Once all of the greens are added, sprinkle in the seasoning salt and ground black pepper.

◆ Add the sliced jalapeño and vinegar, and stir the ingredients. Cover the pot and simmer for 1 hour and 10 minutes over medium heat, stirring occasionally. Let cool slightly and garnish with extra bacon before serving.

Note: When using bunches of greens, be sure to use the scales in the produce section at your local grocery store to make sure you have the right amount.

Turnip and Mustard Greens with Salt Pork

Did I tell y'all that we had greens almost every darn day when I was growing up? Greens were our main vegetable. It was usually collard greens, but when my mom wanted to be fancy, she'd make turnip and mustard greens with salt pork. That was her showing off her skills, demonstrating that she could do more than just the everyday greens. The salt pork in this doesn't have the smokiness of the bacon ends or ham hocks, but it infuses the greens with a pure porky flavor. And since mustard greens are a tad bit bitter, there's no need to add any vinegar to these.

MAKES 8 TO 10 SERVINGS

12 ounces salt pork, sliced

1 medium yellow onion, diced

10 to 12 cups vegetable broth (depending on how much liquid you like)

3 bunches mustard greens, cleaned and cut (see opposite page)

6 bunches turnip greens, cleaned and cut (see opposite page)

2 teaspoons seasoning salt

1 teaspoon coarse black pepper

1 teaspoon red pepper flakes

1 tablespoon brown sugar

2 medium turnips, peeled and chopped

◆ In a large pot over medium heat, add the salt pork slices. Cook for 5 to 7 minutes, or until it browns, then add in the onions. Cook for 2 more minutes.

◆ Pour in the vegetable broth and slowly start adding in the greens. Once all the greens are in the pot, sprinkle in the seasoning salt, black pepper, and red pepper flakes. Give everything a good stir and add the sugar.

◆ Reduce the heat to medium low, place a lid on top of the pot, and let the greens simmer for about 1½ hours.

◆ After the time has passed, add in the chopped turnips and cook for 30 more minutes. Serve with cornbread.

Note: Yes! I added brown sugar. It will not make the greens sweet; it will simply help bring the bitter notes from the mustard greens down.

Cleaning Greens 101

When I was a little girl, we had greens every single night with dinner and I hated them! Now, I love the hearty mix of smoked meat and leafy greens—but I don't love the cleaning process. Still, it's essential, so don't try to find a way around it.

Yes, even the "precleaned" ones need more cleaning before you can begin cooking them. Start by separating all the leaves and tossing them into a clean sink (I usually bleach my sink down before cleaning my greens). Once the leaves are in the sink, rinse them well, mixing them to get off any dirt. Next, fill the sink with lukewarm water, 1 tablespoon salt, and ¼ cup apple cider vinegar. Let the greens soak for 30 minutes, then rub the leaves using your fingertips. Drain the water and rinse the leaves. Repeat the steps until the sink is grit- and dirt-free.

Now you're ready to start chopping them. For leaves with a thick stem, I fold each leaf in half so that the rib—extending from the stem all the way up the leaf—runs along one edge, then cut that out and compost it. Stack a few of the leaves at a time and chop those up into the desired size.

Smothered Potatoes and Sausage

FAN FAVE!

I call this an anytime meal because you can have it all day long. If you have it for breakfast, you can crack an egg over top; if you have it for dinner, you can serve it with cornbread and your favorite vegetable. It's pretty quick, and there are just a few special things I do to make it turn out well. When I'm slicing the potatoes, I make sure to do it all evenly, so they cook at the same time. If you have some big chunks, the smaller pieces will fall apart before the big ones soften. The other thing I do is fry the sausage in the oil, then take it out while I cook everything else. That gives the smoky flavor to the oil and vegetables without overcooking the meat. Then I just toss it back in right at the end. Tip: To prevent browning, set the potatoes to the side in a large bowl with water while you prepare the other ingredients.

MAKES 6 SERVINGS

Scant ½ cup vegetable oil

1 pound smoked sausage, sliced

5 to 6 medium russet potatoes, washed, peeled, and sliced

1 large yellow onion, sliced

1 large green bell pepper, sliced

2 teaspoons garlic powder

2 teaspoons kosher salt

1 teaspoon ground black pepper

¾ cup chicken broth

Chopped fresh parsley, for garnish

- In a large skillet over medium heat, heat the vegetable oil. When the skillet is hot, add the sausage and cook until browned, 5 to 7 minutes. Remove the sausage, reserving the oil in the pan.

- Pat the potatoes dry, then add them to the skillet. Fry for 5 to 8 minutes, or until tender. Once the potatoes are nice and tender, add the onion and bell pepper. Sprinkle in the garlic powder, salt, and pepper. Stir.

- Add the chicken broth and toss the smoked sausage back into the pan. Stir the ingredients. Cook until everything is nice and tender, and the broth is absorbed by the potatoes. Garnish with chopped parsley.

Fried Cabbage

It's no secret that I love cabbage. I like braised cabbage (page 106) and cabbage rolls (page 182). My mom would make fried cabbage for us on nights when she didn't have too much time, because it cooks up just a little quicker than collard greens, and I would secretly be so happy. Because you're basically just frying the cabbage in bacon ends with onions and bell peppers, it packs a powerful punch of flavor that can rival those collard greens. But you still need the cornbread on the side (you always need the cornbread).

MAKES 6 SERVINGS

½ pound thick-cut bacon, cut in small pieces	3 garlic cloves, minced
1 large head of cabbage (about 3 pounds), sliced and washed	1 tablespoon onion powder
	1 tablespoon garlic powder
1 large red bell pepper, diced	1½ teaspoons kosher salt
1 large green bell pepper, diced	½ teaspoon ground black pepper
1 large yellow onion, diced	¼ teaspoon red pepper flakes

◆ In a large pot or saucepan over medium heat, brown the bacon. Cook until most of the fat is rendered, about 7 minutes. Remove the bacon and set to the side.

◆ In the same pan, add the cabbage, bell peppers, onion, and garlic cloves. *Note: Everything will not fit into the pot at first. Once it cooks down, it will shrink!* Cook until the cabbage and other ingredients start to get tender, about 10 minutes.

◆ Sprinkle in the onion and garlic powders, salt, black pepper, and red pepper flakes. Cook for another 5 minutes or so, then toss in the bacon. Stir the ingredients, then add everything into your serving dish.

Braised Cabbage with Smoked Turkey

◇◇

Everybody likes their cabbage a different texture, but my favorite is when it's super soft and tender, like it's lost any ability to hold itself up. That's where this braised cabbage recipe comes in: the vegetables get to take a nice, slow bath in chicken broth with smoked turkey wings, letting all that meaty flavor absorb right into the leaves. It barely needs any other seasoning, because it just soaks that all up and delivers it straight to your plate.

MAKES 6 SERVINGS

8 cups chicken broth
1 large smoked turkey wing
2 tablespoons extra-virgin olive oil
1 large yellow onion, diced

1 large head of green cabbage, rinsed, chopped, and outer leaves discarded
2 teaspoons seasoning salt
½ teaspoon ground black pepper
½ teaspoon red pepper flakes

◆ In a large pot over high heat, add the chicken broth and smoked turkey wing. Cover the pot with a lid, and let the turkey wing boil until it starts to fall off the bone, usually around 45 minutes.

◆ In a medium skillet over medium heat, drizzle in the olive oil. Add in the onion and cook until tender, about 3 minutes. Turn off the heat, then set to the side.

◆ Remove the lid from the pot with the turkey wing and add the cabbage and onion. Sprinkle in the salt, pepper, and red pepper flakes. Stir. Cook the cabbage for about 20 minutes, or until it reaches your preferred tenderness.

Okra and Tomatoes

◇◇

Okra and tomatoes go together like ham hocks and greens—they grow right alongside each other in the South, coming ripe in the same season, and pair up on the plate perfectly. While we mostly had fried okra growing up, when I was back visiting family, we'd sometimes sit down to a summer lunch of a big bowl of stewed okra and tomatoes with a little cornbread on the side. These days, I like to put it over rice and serve it with my Beef Meatloaf (page 155).

MAKES 6 TO 8 SERVINGS

2 tablespoons olive oil	1 tablespoon brown sugar
½ yellow onion, diced	1½ teaspoons kosher salt
3 garlic cloves, minced	½ teaspoon ground black pepper
2 (14.5-ounce) cans diced tomatoes	2 sprigs of fresh thyme
1 pound fresh okra, sliced in quarters	½ cup vegetable broth
1 tablespoon salted butter	1 tablespoon cornstarch

◆ In a large saucepan over medium heat, drizzle in the olive oil. Once the oil is hot, add the onion and cook for 5 minutes.

◆ Add the garlic and cook for 1 minute before adding the diced tomatoes. Be sure *not* to strain the tomatoes. You want the juice as well!

◆ Add the okra, butter, sugar, salt, pepper, and thyme. Stir the ingredients, then cook for 20 minutes.

◆ Pour the vegetable broth into a liquid measuring cup, then sprinkle in the cornstarch. Whisk until lump-free and add to the pan with the okra and tomatoes. Cook for 5 minutes, then serve and enjoy!

Cheesy Tomato Pie

Y'all already know how much I love lasagna, so when I sat down to dinner in Baton Rouge and someone served me this dish that was like a Southern spin on it, you know I fell in love. The crushed Ritz crackers on the bottom just soak up all the great tomato juices, and the layer on top gives it a buttery, crunchy crust. In between, it's all melty, creamy, cheesy greatness.

MAKES 8 SERVINGS

Vegetable oil, for greasing
3 tablespoons extra-virgin olive oil
1 large yellow onion, diced
2 pounds roma tomatoes, diced
2 tablespoons chopped fresh basil
2 teaspoons kosher salt
1 teaspoon chopped fresh thyme

½ teaspoon ground black pepper
2 cups mayonnaise
2 cups shredded sharp cheddar cheese
1 cup shredded Havarti cheese
2½ sleeves of Ritz crackers, crushed, divided

- Preheat the oven to 350 degrees F. Lightly oil a 9-by-13-inch baking dish.

- In a large sauté pan over medium-high heat, drizzle in the olive oil. Once the oil is hot, add the onions and cook until tender, 3 to 5 minutes.

- Next, add in the tomatoes, basil, salt, thyme, and pepper. Stir. Cook for 15 minutes, then turn off the heat and set the pan to the side.

- In a large mixing bowl, combine the mayonnaise, cheddar, and Havarti. Set aside.

- In the baking dish, sprinkle ⅓ of the crushed Ritz crackers (save 1 cup for the topping!). Make sure that it is spread evenly on the bottom. Pour half of the tomato mixture on top of the Ritz crackers. Repeat the layers.

- Top the layers with the mayonnaise-and-cheese mixture and smooth out. Sprinkle the remaining 1 cup crushed Ritz on top. Bake uncovered for 45 minutes. Remove from the oven and let sit for 15 minutes before serving.

Pinto Beans and Ham Hocks

FAN FAVE!

◇◇◇◇◇◇◇◇◇◇◇◇◇◇◇◇◇◇◇◇◇◇◇◇◇◇◇◇◇◇◇◇◇◇◇◇◇◇◇

When I tell you that I was raised on beans and rice, I truly mean it. We would make one big pot at the beginning of the week and eat it all week long. It was cheap and easy—and it still is. The slow cooker is my lifesaver when I'm cooking beans because I don't have to remember to soak the dried beans; I can just toss them in and they soften as they cook. The ham hock meat falls off the bone and mixes into the beans, perfect for serving over rice when they're done.

MAKES 8 SERVINGS

1 large ham hock or smoked turkey wing

7 cups water

3 cups dry pinto beans, sorted and washed

1 medium yellow onion, diced

1 tablespoon minced garlic

2 teaspoons seasoning salt

½ teaspoon ground black pepper

Chopped green onions, for garnish (optional)

2 to 2½ cups steamed rice

◆ Add the ham hock, water, beans, onion, garlic, salt, and pepper to a 6-quart slow cooker. Set on high, cover, and cook for 6 hours.

◆ Once the beans are done, garnish with green onions and serve over rice.

Dry Beans

Let's talk about dry beans. Some people make them with ease, while others shy away from making them. They aren't hard to prepare, but there are a few things that you should know before making them. For one, you have to sort and clean them before cooking them. You'd be surprised how many people skip this step! Be sure to open up the bag of beans and place the beans on a flat surface. Go through the beans and pick out all the rotten ones—there also might be some pebbles in the bunch that need to be discarded. After that, rinse the beans with cool water because beans are a tad bit dirty. Last but not least, you can decide on whether or not you want to soak the beans. I personally don't soak my beans all the time, and there really isn't a huge difference (in my humble opinion) in the outcome if you cook them long enough. There are different options for soaking (look on the back of the bag of your beans), but when I do soak the beans, I usually do a quick soak because I don't have time to wait 8 hours for beans!

Here's how to quick soak them: Bring a big pot of water to a boil and add the beans. As soon as you add them, turn the burner off, remove the pot from the heat, and cover it. Let those soak for 2 hours, then drain them and you're ready to cook!

Red Beans and Rice

Popeyes, take a seat, there are some new beans in town! This recipe has everything: a quick-soak method to get your beans going fast, the spice of andouille sausage, and plenty of garlic and thyme. The red beans don't need much else, because they're cooked in chicken broth and enhanced with the andouille, so they come out full of flavor. When it comes to serving, I put together a big bowl of beans, add a scoop of rice, then pile a little more beans on top. Then I serve it with Southern Fried Chicken (page 158) because red beans and rice goes with fried chicken like peanut butter with jelly.

MAKES 6 SERVINGS

1 (16-ounce) bag dry red kidney beans, sorted and rinsed

6 cups chicken broth

2 tablespoons extra-virgin olive oil

1 pound andouille sausage, sliced into ¼-inch pieces

½ medium red onion, diced

½ medium red bell pepper, diced

2 garlic cloves, minced

2½ teaspoons Creole seasoning

1 teaspoon ground black pepper

2 sprigs of fresh thyme

3 cups steamed rice

- In a large pot over high heat, bring about 4 cups of water to a boil. Add the beans, cover, and turn off the heat. Let the beans sit for 30 minutes.

- When the time has passed, drain the water and pour the chicken broth into the pot with the beans. Turn the heat to medium, cover, and simmer for 20 to 25 minutes.

- In a medium skillet over medium heat, drizzle in the olive oil. Once the oil is hot, add the sausage and cook until browned, 5 to 7 minutes. Add the onion and pepper, and cook for 2 minutes. Add the garlic. Cook for another 5 minutes, then turn off the heat.

- Add the sausage, onion, pepper, and garlic into the pot with the beans. Sprinkle in the Creole seasoning and black pepper, and toss in the thyme. Stir the ingredients, and simmer for 1 hour and 30 minutes. Be sure to stir occasionally while the beans are cooking so nothing burns at the bottom! Once done, serve with steamed rice.

Soul Food Style Lima Beans

All beans were not created equal, because nothing comforts quite like a lima bean. Something about the way the bean breaks down as it cooks makes them end up as creamy as Grandma's grits. And because of the bacon I cook them with, all that creaminess is infused with pure smoky flavor. I like to serve mine over rice.

MAKES 6 SERVINGS

1 (16-ounce) bag of large dry lima beans, sorted and rinsed	6 cups chicken broth
½ pound thick-cut bacon	2 teaspoons granulated sugar
½ medium yellow onion, diced	2 teaspoons kosher salt
1 tablespoon minced garlic	½ teaspoon ground black pepper
	Chopped fresh parsley, for garnish

♦ In a large stockpot over high heat, add the beans and about 6 cups water. Once the water starts to boil, turn off the heat and let the lima beans sit for 30 minutes. Then drain the water out of the pot and set the beans to the side.

♦ In a large skillet over medium-high heat, cook the bacon until it's nice and crisp. Remove the bacon from the skillet but keep the bacon drippings in the pan. Add the onion and cook until tender. Add the garlic and cook for 2 more minutes, then turn off the heat.

♦ Put the pot with the lima beans over medium heat, and pour in the chicken broth. Add the onion and garlic to the pot, and stir. Crumble in the bacon, then sprinkle in the sugar, salt, and pepper. Stir the ingredients and cover the pot with a lid.

♦ Simmer over medium-high heat for 35 to 45 minutes, or until the beans are nice and creamy. Garnish with parsley and serve alone or over rice.

Baked Beans

You can't have a cookout without baked beans; they're absolutely essential—they're the soul of a soul food barbecue. But I've got a confession: I cheat when I make mine. I like to use canned pork and beans because there's just no better way to get the intensely unified flavor of the meat and beans together. That's only the base, though; they still need plenty of my own spin on them to get up to my standards. I cook them up with smoked sausage, lots of onions and peppers, molasses, and Worcestershire sauce. The result is sweet and smoky, and everybody wants to know my secret. I just smile and vow to never let them into my kitchen to find out.

MAKES 6 TO 8 SERVINGS

1 tablespoon vegetable oil, plus more for greasing	¼ cup ketchup
	¼ cup brown sugar
½ pound smoked sausage, diced	2 tablespoons yellow mustard
½ red onion, diced	2 tablespoons maple syrup
1 medium green bell pepper, diced	2 tablespoons molasses
1 (28-ounce) can pork and beans	1 tablespoon Worcestershire sauce

---

◆ Preheat the oven to 350 degrees F. Lightly oil a 9-by-13-inch baking dish.

◆ In a large skillet over medium-high heat, drizzle in the vegetable oil. Add the smoked sausage and cook until it browns. Add the onion and bell pepper. Cook until tender, then turn off the heat.

◆ In the baking dish, add the pork and beans. Next add the sausage, onion, bell pepper, ketchup, sugar, mustard, maple syrup, molasses, and Worcestershire sauce. Mix until well combined. Bake uncovered for 1 hour, then serve.

Cornbread Dressing

✧✧✧✧✧✧✧✧✧✧✧✧✧✧✧✧✧✧✧✧✧✧✧✧✧✧✧✧✧✧✧✧✧✧

Cornbread dressing is what some people might call stuffing, except that in my family we never stuffed it into anything—I think because then we would have been limited on how much would fit!

For this recipe, start by making the Sweet Cornbread recipe (page 122), but omit the sugar. Use that to make the dressing, along with a sleeve of crackers to add a little more texture. Try serving this dressing with my Fried Ribs (page 138), or at Thanksgiving dinner.

MAKES 8 TO 10 SERVINGS

Vegetable oil, for greasing
2 tablespoons extra-virgin olive oil
1 large yellow onion, diced
3 stalks celery, chopped
5 garlic cloves, minced
5 fresh sage leaves, finely chopped, or 2½ teaspoons ground sage
1 batch cornbread (use the recipe on page 122, but be sure to omit the sugar!)

1 sleeve Ritz or saltine crackers
4 to 6 cups chicken broth
1 (14-ounce) can cream of chicken soup
3 eggs, lightly beaten
2 teaspoons seasoning salt
1 teaspoon coarse black pepper
1 teaspoon dried thyme

◆ Preheat the oven to 350 degrees F. Lightly oil a 9-by-13-inch baking dish.

◆ In a large nonstick pan over medium heat, drizzle in the olive oil. Once the oil is hot, add the onion, celery, and garlic. Cook until nice and tender. Toss in the sage and cook for another 2 minutes. Turn off the heat.

◆ In a large mixing bowl, crumble the cornbread and the crackers. Add the cooked vegetables, chicken broth, cream of chicken soup, and eggs. Mix well. Sprinkle in the seasoning salt, pepper, and thyme, and mix again.

◆ In the baking dish, pour in the dressing mixture. Bake uncovered for about 45 minutes. Cool slightly before serving.

Succotash

◇◇◇

Succotash is as fun to make as it is to say—even though it's really just a fancy name for what I do when I have a whole bunch of vegetables sitting around in my refrigerator and freezer and need to use them up! Lima beans, corn, and tomatoes are the base of a good succotash, but everything else can just depend on what you need to use up before it goes bad. But no matter what you do, it always ends up as a big, quick, and colorful side dish.

MAKES 6 SERVINGS

1 pound frozen lima beans, thawed

3 cups vegetable broth

8 slices thick-cut bacon

2 cups frozen or fresh corn

½ medium red onion, diced

½ medium green bell pepper, diced

½ medium red bell pepper, diced

2 teaspoons seasoning salt

½ teaspoon ground black pepper

¼ teaspoon red pepper flakes

3 small roma tomatoes, diced

+ In a medium pot over high heat, bring the lima beans and vegetable broth to a boil. Boil the lima beans for about 10 minutes, then remove the beans from the broth and set them to the side. Be sure to reserve 1 cup of the broth.

+ Place a large sauté pan over medium heat and add the bacon. Fry the bacon until it's nice and crisp, then remove it from the pan. Leave the fat behind.

+ In the same pan, add the corn and fry for about 5 minutes, then add the onion and bell peppers. Fry for about 2 more minutes. Add the seasoning salt, black pepper, and red pepper flakes. Stir the ingredients, then add in the lima beans and reserved 1 cup of vegetable broth.

+ Chop up the bacon that you cooked earlier and toss it into the pan. Cook for another 5 minutes, then add the tomatoes. Give everything a nice stir before serving.

Sweet Cornbread

You can't have soul food without some type of cornbread—it's a cheap staple and goes with everything. I eat it with beans and rice, gumbo, and my greens. I even like to have it for breakfast with a big glass of milk. It is one of the mainstays in my kitchen, and I could probably make it with my eyes closed. And when you're cooking from my book, you'll want to keep this handy because it goes with just about everything in it.

Now, I personally love sweet cornbread, even though I know a lot of people (even some in my own family!) will say it's not Southern cornbread if it's sweet. We'll just have to agree to disagree, because I like everything sweet and that goes double for my cornbread. That said, you can make this exact same recipe without the sugar and it will work just fine—and that's what I do when I'm making it to put into my Cornbread Dressing (page 119).

MAKES 10 TO 12 SERVINGS

½ cup vegetable oil, plus more for greasing

3 cups all-purpose flour

1 cup yellow cornmeal

1 cup granulated sugar

½ cup brown sugar

1 tablespoon baking powder

1 teaspoon kosher salt

4 medium eggs

2½ cups whole milk

1 cup (2 sticks) salted butter, softened

◆ Preheat the oven to 350 degrees F. Lightly oil a 9-by-13-inch baking dish or a 12-inch cast-iron skillet.

◆ In a large mixing bowl, combine the flour, cornmeal, sugars, baking powder, and salt. Once the dry ingredients are well incorporated, add the eggs, milk, butter, and vegetable oil. Mix everything until it's combined.

◆ Pour the cornbread batter into the baking dish or skillet, and bake for 35 to 40 minutes. Serve with Red Beans and Rice (page 114).

Hush Puppies

When I was about seven, we were down in Louisiana and one of my cousins was having a fish fry. Now, we ate plenty of fried fish up here in Seattle, but we always served it with cornbread. Down there, when they dropped the seafood in the fryer, they also added these delightful dough balls. And little seven-year-old me was blown away. We just never had hush puppies in the Northwest—at least before that. You better believe I came back and set right on figuring out how to make them.

I add finely diced onion and plenty of seasoning to get the flavor right and use self-rising flour to make sure they come out crispy on the outside, light and fluffy in the middle. They're a classic with seafood, so you'll want to cook them when you're already deep-frying something like Deep-Fried Catfish (page 171) or Cajun Fried Shrimp and Oysters (page 166).

MAKES 24 HUSH PUPPIES

1 cup yellow cornmeal	1 small yellow onion, finely diced
1 cup self-rising flour	3 to 4 green onions, finely diced
2 tablespoons granulated sugar	1 cup buttermilk
1 teaspoon garlic powder	1 egg
½ teaspoon kosher salt	2 cups vegetable oil, for
½ teaspoon cayenne pepper	deep-frying

◆ In a large bowl, combine the cornmeal, flour, sugar, garlic powder, salt, and cayenne pepper. Whisk until everything is lump-free, then add the onions, buttermilk, and egg. Mix the ingredients until well combined, but don't overmix.

◆ In a large stockpot over medium heat, add the oil. Once the oil is hot, start spooning in about 2 tablespoons of the batter, 4 to 5 hush puppies at a time. Fry the hush puppies until they are a nice golden brown, 3 to 4 minutes. Remove them from the oil and place them on a paper-towel-lined plate before serving.

Red Rice

◇◇

We had red rice at a family reunion in the South, but I never realized how popular it was, because we didn't make it much in the Northwest. But years later, a coworker of mine in Seattle made it for a potluck, and it brought back all kinds of great memories—but the rice itself was not quite as good. So I had to get into the kitchen and figure out what my cousins back in Louisiana had been doing right. The answer is using plenty of smoked sausage, bell pepper, and seasoning salt—and just a touch of brown sugar for sweetness.

MAKES 8 TO 12 SERVINGS

Vegetable oil, for greasing

1 pound bacon, chopped

1 pound smoked sausage, sliced in ½-inch rounds

1 large red onion, diced

1 large green bell pepper, diced

3 cups chicken broth

6 ounces tomato paste

1 tablespoon brown sugar

2½ teaspoons seasoning salt

2 teaspoons garlic powder

1 teaspoon ground black pepper

2 cups uncooked rice

1 bunch green onions, chopped

◆ Preheat the oven to 350 degrees F. Lightly oil a 4-quart casserole dish.

◆ In a large stockpot over medium heat, cook the bacon until it's nice and crisp. Remove the bacon from the pot and set aside, but be sure to leave the bacon drippings behind. Add the smoked sausage to the pot and cook for about 5 minutes. Then add the bacon back in, along with the onion and bell pepper. Cook until tender, 3 to 5 minutes.

◆ Add the chicken broth, tomato paste, and sugar. Stir until well combined, then sprinkle in the seasoning salt, garlic powder, and black pepper. Add the rice and stir again. Simmer for 15 minutes over medium-high heat.

◆ In the casserole dish, add the red rice mixture. Cover and place in the oven for 35 to 40 minutes. Once finished, remove from the oven, uncover, and stir. Let cool and top with green onions before serving.

Pull-Apart Yeast Rolls

◇◇◇

When I was growing up, one of my aunts always had the reputation for making the best yeast rolls—we had to have them every Thanksgiving. But then one year, my cousin and I were playing around and walked into the kitchen to witness her pulling them straight out of the package! Even as little kids, we knew how embarrassing that would be if anyone found out, so we kept our mouths shut because we knew what was good for us. But that's always been my motivation to make these when I think I don't want to spend the time kneading and resting the dough—I don't want to be the one caught pulling them straight from the package! So I make them myself, and I'm always glad I did when I pull the warm, light, fluffy rolls out of the oven—and they are even better than hers were!

MAKES 9 LARGE ROLLS

Vegetable oil, for greasing	6 cups all-purpose flour, plus more to knead
1¼ cups warm water, divided	
½ cup granulated sugar	2 teaspoons kosher salt
5 teaspoons active dry yeast	3 eggs, at room temperature, divided
½ cup whole milk, warm	½ cup unsalted butter, melted

◆ Lightly grease a large bowl and a 9-by-13-inch baking dish.

◆ In a medium bowl, combine ¼ cup of the warm water, the sugar, and the yeast. Mix and let it sit for 5 minutes until the yeast foams. Add in the rest of the warm water and warm milk, then set to the side.

◆ In a large bowl, sift the flour and salt. Set aside.

◆ In a small bowl, lightly beat 2 of the eggs. Add the beaten eggs and the yeast mixture into the bowl with the dry ingredients. Mix everything using your hands, or use a handheld mixer with dough hook attachment. If using a handheld mixer, mix on low speed.

CONTINUED

- Knead the dough on a lightly floured surface for about 10 minutes. Place the dough into the greased bowl and cover with a clean cloth or towel. Let it rest for 1½ hours in a warm, draft-free place.

- When the dough has risen, punch the middle to remove air. Then separate and form 9 rolls out of the dough. Place the rolls in the baking dish, leaving an inch or so between each one. Cover with a clean towel and let them rise for about 30 to 45 minutes, at which time the rolls should have doubled in size. Preheat the oven to 350 degrees F.

- Separate the yolk from the remaining egg, and brush the egg white on top of the rolls. Bake for 15 to 20 minutes, then remove the rolls from the oven and brush with your desired amount of melted butter. Pull the rolls apart, serve with even more butter, and enjoy.

The Star of the Soul Food Supper

Oven-Baked BBQ Ribs

My mom never grilled when I was growing up, so BBQ always meant the oven to us at home. Now that I'm grown up—and still live in the rainy Northwest—I think I have a few guesses as to why she did that. We grill outside sometimes, but I've learned from her, and with this recipe you can't even tell the difference—you have so much more control over the heat when you're inside, it might even be better than smoking outside. Don't forget to serve these ribs with some of my Southern Potato Salad (page 95), and it's just like the cookout, minus worrying about the weather.

MAKES 8 TO 10 SERVINGS

6 pounds Saint Louis style ribs, membrane removed

2 tablespoons vegetable oil

¼ cup brown sugar

2 tablespoons freshly ground black pepper

2 tablespoons smoked, sweet, or regular paprika

2 tablespoons onion powder

2 tablespoons garlic powder

1 tablespoon kosher salt

2 teaspoons dried parsley flakes

1½ teaspoons dry mustard

1½ teaspoons red pepper flakes

1 tablespoon hickory liquid smoke

1½ tablespoons apple cider vinegar

BBQ sauce

◆ Preheat the oven to 375 degrees F.

◆ In a 9-by-13-inch baking dish, add the ribs and drizzle the oil all over the front and back of them. Sprinkle on the sugar, black pepper, paprika, onion and garlic powders, salt, parsley, mustard, and red pepper flakes. Drizzle the liquid smoke and vinegar over the ribs, and brush or rub them down until they are thoroughly covered.

◆ Cover the ribs with aluminum foil, and bake for 1 hour and 20 minutes. Remove the ribs from the oven and remove the foil.

◆ Brush your favorite BBQ sauce on the ribs, and turn the oven on broil. Broil the ribs until the sauce is nice and sticky, 3 to 5 minutes. Remove from the oven and let sit for 5 minutes before serving.

Fried Ribs

◇◇

When I was about eight years old, this guy opened a rib joint in the Central District in Seattle, not far from where we lived, and he specialized in fried ribs. They were the absolute best thing you ever tasted, but the owner was so rude that my mom refused to go back and get his amazing food. Instead, she decided to learn how to make fried ribs herself, and I was right there with her, watching her play around in the kitchen until she got it right. When I got older, I took her recipe and perfected it—maybe even better than Mr. Mean's version.

MAKES 8 SERVINGS

4 pounds extra-tender pork ribs, membrane removed

For the brine:
8 cups cold water
4 tablespoons granulated sugar
2 tablespoons kosher salt

For the ribs:
½ cup mild hot sauce
1½ cups self-rising flour
2½ teaspoons seasoning salt
2 teaspoons onion powder
2 teaspoons garlic powder
2 teaspoons paprika
1½ teaspoons ground black pepper
½ teaspoon cayenne pepper
2 cups vegetable oil, for deep-frying

◆ Cut the ribs into sections and place them in a large bowl. Set to the side.

◆ In a separate large bowl, combine the water, sugar, and salt. Stir until the salt and sugar dissolve, then pour the brine all over the ribs. Cover the bowl and refrigerate overnight (6 to 8 hours), then drain. Once you drain the brine from the ribs, don't rinse them.

◆ Pour hot sauce all over the ribs and make sure that they are well coated. Set the ribs to the side.

◆ Grab a large freezer bag and add in the flour, seasoning salt, onion powder, garlic powder, paprika, black pepper, and cayenne pepper. Shake the bag to make sure that everything is well incorporated. Start adding the ribs to the bag and shake the bag to coat them. Repeat the shaking process twice to ensure that you have a nice coating! Place coated ribs on a baking sheet.

- In a deep-frying pan or deep fryer, pour enough oil to cover ribs by about ½ inch. Heat the oil to 360 degrees F.

- Slowly start adding in the ribs. If you're using a deep-frying pan, be sure to turn the ribs every 3 to 5 minutes. Fry each batch for about 15 minutes until they are golden brown. Once done, place the fried ribs on a paper-towel-lined baking sheet. Serve with your favorite hot sauce.

Lemon Pepper and Honey Country Ribs

In my childhood home, we had a giant deep freezer that was like a treasure trove of whatever meats my mom had bought when they were on sale. It was wide and flat and full of turkey wings and pork chops, and I hated having to dig around in it! So when it was my turn to figure out what to make, I usually just chose whatever was on top. Thankfully, one thing I could always count on being right up there was some country ribs.

Over the years I've played around with different recipes for this cut of meat, but this one is a favorite because the simple wet rub with the bitter of the lemon pepper pairs so well with the sweet honey glaze.

MAKES 6 SERVINGS

Vegetable oil, for greasing	1 tablespoon minced garlic
¼ cup yellow mustard	2 teaspoons paprika
2 tablespoons brown sugar	2 pounds pork country ribs
2 tablespoons minced yellow onion	¼ cup honey
1½ tablespoons lemon pepper	1 tablespoon cornstarch

◆ Preheat the oven to 325 degrees F. Lightly oil a 9-by-13-inch baking dish, then set to the side.

◆ In a small bowl, combine the mustard, sugar, onion, lemon pepper, garlic, and paprika.

◆ In a large bowl or on a flat surface, rub the mustard mixture all over the ribs. Put the ribs in the baking dish and cover with aluminum foil. Bake in the oven for 1 hour. Remove from the oven and uncover.

◆ In a small bowl or large cup, pour the liquid from the bottom of the baking dish. Add the honey and cornstarch, and mix until lump-free. Pour the honey mixture over the ribs. Bake again in the oven, uncovered, another 1½ hours, and be sure to baste every 30 minutes with the liquid from the bottom of the pan. Remove from the oven and let cool before serving.

Slow Cooker BBQ Pulled Pork

Some people might call this a cheater's pulled pork because I don't use a grill or smoker, but my aunt Sandy made the best pulled pork ever, and she did hers in the oven. I don't have time for the smoker or the oven, so I stick mine in the slow cooker and let the machine do the work. In my world, it's not cheating if it turns out delicious, and this turns out just like it would on the grill. You can use it for all the same things you would a traditional pulled pork—I like to make it into sandwiches with hamburger buns and a little Coleslaw (page 97).

MAKES 6 SERVINGS

2 to 3 pounds pork shoulder roast	2 tablespoons smoked paprika
1 tablespoon vegetable oil	2 teaspoons kosher salt
2 tablespoons liquid smoke	1 teaspoon ground black pepper
2 teaspoons apple cider vinegar	1 teaspoon mustard powder
¼ cup dark brown sugar	1 to 1½ cups hickory BBQ sauce

◆ On a large baking sheet, place the roast and drizzle the vegetable oil all over it, followed by the liquid smoke and vinegar.

◆ In a small bowl, combine the sugar with the paprika, salt, pepper, and mustard powder. Coat the roast with the spice mix.

◆ Place the roast in a 6-quart slow cooker and cover with the lid. Cook on low for 4 hours.

◆ Shred the meat, and pour in the BBQ sauce. Stir, then cook for an additional 2 hours (still on low). Then serve and enjoy!

Slow Cooker Garlic-Stuffed Pork Roast

◇◇

My friend Brian and I were buddies back at my old job, and we'd always exchange recipes before or after our shifts. I remember him raving about his delicious slow-cooked pork roast and how everyone loved it. But when I finally asked him what was so special about it, he told me, "Garlic! I stuff it with garlic, and I season it with salt and pepper." I thought he had lost his damn mind, because it sounded so bland. Just garlic? Whatever! But I gave it a try anyway (with my own little touch, of course) and you know what, Brian was right. Sadly, he recently passed away, and so every time I make this, I am thankful for the time we spent together—and his sneaky garlic trick.

MAKES 8 TO 10 SERVINGS

3 to 4 pounds boneless pork butt roast

6 to 8 garlic cloves

1 cup chopped green onions

1 (0.75-ounce) package of ranch seasoning

1 teaspoon ground black pepper

2 cups chicken broth

1 pound baby carrots

1 pound red potatoes, washed and chopped

♦ Puncture 6 to 8 holes into the roast and stuff them with the garlic cloves. Carefully place the roast into a 6-quart slow cooker.

♦ Toss in the green onions, then sprinkle the ranch seasoning and black pepper all over the roast. Pour in the chicken broth. Set the slow cooker on high and cook for 2 hours.

♦ Add the carrots and potatoes, stir, and cook for 2 more hours. Serve.

Sunday Supper

For my family and lots of other people growing up, Sunday supper was the most important meal of the week. It was the one day my mom had completely off work, the only time she had to make a really huge meal during the week. She would start cooking early in the morning and cook all day, making smothered oxtails, potato salad, collards, cornbread, and sweet potato pie. We would usually have three aunts, four cousins, and two uncles over for the feast, and there were still leftovers that we could keep and warm up all week. It was our Soul Food Sunday, and it still is in my house. These days, it's usually just three of us—my husband, son, and me—but sometimes we'll have people over, or I'll share with the neighbors. I still like to make a big meal with all the fixings, but unlike my mom, I'm not doubling or tripling every recipe!

Slow Cooker Beef Brisket

FAN FAVE!

◇◇

If you're anything like me, you love beef brisket but hate smoking it for hours. You have to go out (usually in the rain, at least here in the Pacific Northwest) and check on it all the time. Well, I have the solution for that—my slow cooker beef brisket! All you have to do is season it, put it in the slow cooker, and pretty much go on about your day, no need to babysit. Once it's done slow-cooking, you place it in the oven to get some bark on it.

I used to make this and use the leftovers for the Beef Brisket Hash (page 37), but these days when people hear I'm making it, suddenly friends, family, even neighbors start showing up out of nowhere, so I try to stash a little in the fridge that I can use for breakfast the next day.

MAKES 10 TO 12 SERVINGS

2 tablespoons extra-virgin olive oil	2 tablespoons paprika
2 tablespoons apple cider vinegar	1 tablespoon kosher salt
1 tablespoon liquid smoke	1 tablespoon dried parsley flakes
½ cup light brown sugar	1 teaspoon ground black pepper
2 tablespoons garlic powder	1 teaspoon cayenne pepper
2 tablespoons onion powder	7 to 8 pounds beef brisket

◆ In a small mixing bowl, combine the oil, vinegar, liquid smoke, sugar, garlic and onion powders, paprika, salt, parsley, black pepper, and cayenne using a whisk. Rub the mixture all over the brisket.

◆ Spray a 6-quart slow cooker with nonstick cooking spray and place the brisket inside. Set the slow cooker on low and cook for 12 hours.

◆ Line a 9-by-13-inch baking dish with aluminum foil. Once the brisket is done, carefully remove it from the slow cooker and place it in the prepared baking dish. Turn the oven on broil and cook the brisket until the "bark" (the rub) is dark brown, 3 to 5 minutes. Remove the brisket from the oven, cover it with aluminum foil, and let it rest for 1 hour before serving.

Slow Cooker Smothered Oxtails

FAN FAVE!

When the onions and oxtails start simmering, my kitchen fills with the joyous smells of Sunday supper. These oxtails are weekend food through and through, because they have to cook low and slow until the meat slips from the bone and becomes one with the sauce. But even though I do these in the slow cooker now, which means I can go about my whole day and just know that the meat is turning tender and rich, it's still a special ritual to make them, reserved only for days of rest. It's like I can just sense the way the bones are flavoring the broth in that slow cooker and imagine how good it will all be spooned over mashed potatoes and rice.

When it's done, the meat will just melt right in your mouth. You'll want to serve this up with the whole Sunday supper menu I've given on page 237, just like my mom would have, because something this good deserves a full-on feast.

The Star of the Soul Food Supper

♥

149

MAKES 4 SERVINGS

2½ pounds oxtails	¾ cup vegetable oil
2 teaspoons kosher salt	3 cups beef broth or water
1 teaspoon freshly cracked or ground black pepper	1 large yellow onion, sliced
	3 garlic cloves, minced
2 tablespoons Worcestershire sauce	Chopped fresh parsley, for garnish
1¼ cups all-purpose flour, divided	

◆ In a large mixing bowl, season the oxtails with salt and pepper. Drizzle the Worcestershire sauce all over, and toss the oxtails to make sure they are coated. Sprinkle ¼ cup of the flour over the oxtails, and toss again to ensure even coating.

◆ In a large sauté pan over medium heat, pour in the vegetable oil. Once the oil is hot, add the oxtails. Once they are nice and brown, remove them from the pan, and put them in a 6-quart slow cooker while you prepare the gravy. If there are burnt pieces of meat in the pan, pour out the oil, strain, clean the pan, then pour the strained oil back into the pan.

CONTINUED

- Over medium heat, start adding the remaining 1 cup flour into the pan, only a little bit at a time. Whisk continuously. Once the flour is brown, resembling chunky peanut butter, slowly pour in the broth. Whisk while you pour!

- Make sure everything is lump-free, then turn the heat from medium to high. When the gravy reaches a full boil, reduce the heat to medium and add in the onions and garlic. Stir the gravy and do a taste test. Add salt and pepper to taste.

- Turn the heat off and pour the gravy into the slow cooker, covering the oxtails. Set the slow cooker on high and cook for 8 hours. Top with parsley and serve with mashed potatoes or rice.

Smothering

I'm all about comfort food, and there is one technique that I always lean on to make sure that my food is full of comfort: smothering. Smothered foods have rich, thick sauces that blanket the main dish as well as whatever they're served over, like rice, cornbread, or biscuits. You can smother all kinds of meat, vegetables, or seafood.

The Southern technique basically just means that you cook the meat (or whatever you're smothering) in a covered pan with a bit of liquid—not all that different than braising, but with less liquid. It does the same thing as stewing or braising, though: slowly cooks less-tender cuts with a bit of liquid so that they stay moist as they turn tender and flavor the sauce. No matter what you're smothering—oxtails, potatoes and sausage, chicken—the result is always full of flavor and comfort.

Creole Lasagna

◇◇◇

I know what y'all are thinking. *What the heck is Creole lasagna?* Well, let me fill you in. One time I had a craving for lasagna, but I didn't have all my usual ingredients. I had no ground beef, but I had ground pork, so instead of taking my butt to the store, I decided to use what I had! In the middle of making my meat sauce, I also realized that I didn't have any seasoning salt, so I decided to use some Creole seasoning instead. To make a long story short, this ended up being some of the best lasagna that I ever made! My husband and son loved it and after that, they requested my "Creole Lasagna" regularly—they won't settle for the traditional kind anymore!

MAKES 10 SERVINGS

Vegetable oil, for greasing

1 pound ground Italian sausage, mild or hot

1 pound ground pork

1 large red bell pepper, diced

1 medium red onion, diced

5 garlic cloves, minced

2 (28-ounce) cans crushed tomatoes, or 8 cups fresh tomatoes, diced

1 tablespoon brown sugar

2½ teaspoons Creole seasoning

2 teaspoons dried basil

1 teaspoon ground black pepper

16 ounces whole-milk ricotta cheese

2 eggs

2 cups shredded mozzarella cheese

12 oven-ready lasagna noodles (see note)

4 cups shredded sharp cheddar cheese

2 cups shredded Colby Jack cheese

Chopped fresh parsley, for garnish

- Preheat the oven to 350 degrees F. Lightly grease a 9-by-13-inch baking dish.

- In a medium bowl, combine the sausage and pork.

- In a large sauté pan over medium heat, cook the sausage-and-pork mixture until it browns. Be sure to break up the meat while it cooks! Remove the meat from the pan and leave about 1½ tablespoons of the grease. Set the meat to the side.

CONTINUED

- Place the pan back on the stove top, still over medium heat, and toss in the peppers and onions. Cook until they soften, then add in the garlic. Return the meat to the pan and add in the tomatoes. Mix the ingredients until everything is well combined. Then add in the sugar, Creole seasoning, basil, and black pepper. Mix the seasonings in, turn the heat down to medium low, and cook for 15 minutes.

- In a large bowl, combine the ricotta, eggs, and mozzarella cheese and mix the ingredients until well combined. Set to the side.

- In the prepared baking dish, add a little of the meat sauce to the bottom. Add a layer of lasagna noodles, then spread a layer of the ricotta mixture over the pasta. Add a layer of the meat sauce, and another layer of the ricotta. Repeat. Add a final layer of pasta, then sauce, then smother with the cheddar and Colby Jack cheeses. Cover loosely with aluminum foil and place in the oven for 1 hour and 15 minutes. Remove from the oven, garnish with parsley, and let sit for 10 minutes before serving.

Note: Although I use oven-ready lasagna noodles, you can certainly use regular. Just be sure to prepare the pasta as directed on the package.

Creole Seasoning versus Cajun Seasoning

Whenever I use Creole or Cajun seasonings in a dish, people ask what the difference is. Outside of the South, people might not understand, but Cajun food comes from the folks who lived way out in rural Louisiana, where they made food from what was around them. Creole food comes from the port cities, where there was a lot of stuff happening—boats coming in and out with lots of fresh herbs and tomatoes. So there is a huge difference in what they need to season their food. Basically, Cajun seasoning is much more spicy! Cajun seasoning consists of a lot of peppers, such as black pepper, cayenne pepper, and sometimes white pepper. It does have other spices as well, but it is mostly made of pepper. Creole seasoning, on the other hand, is much gentler, made up of herbs, usually consisting of thyme, basil, paprika, garlic, and a few others. But really, you don't need to think too much about it, because I suggest you buy yours at the store, so they're each labeled—I use Tone's for Cajun seasoning and Tony Chachere's for Creole seasoning.

Oxtail Stew

◇◇

Oxtails used to be the cheapest meat on the market, so we would have them all the time—along with pig feet, neck bones, and all the other things rich folks wouldn't buy. One batch of this stew would last us for days, and when it seemed like we were running out, my mom would just add more tomatoes and onions to stretch it out for another meal or two. It already has meat and potatoes and carrots in the dish, so it could be a full meal alone, but I like to serve it with my Fried Cabbage (page 105) on the side for a little more green.

MAKES 6 TO 8 SERVINGS

½ cup all-purpose flour

3½ teaspoons seasoning salt

2 teaspoons paprika

½ teaspoon ground black pepper

4 pounds oxtails, fat trimmed

¼ cup vegetable oil

1 large yellow onion, chopped

1 (14.5-ounce) can diced tomatoes, or
    4 large fresh roma tomatoes, diced

4 garlic cloves

3 sprigs of fresh thyme

3 bay leaves

1 (6-ounce) can tomato paste

1 quart (32 ounces) beef broth

1 pound baby carrots

1½ pounds baby red potatoes, chopped

- Grab a large ziplock freezer bag, and add in the flour, seasoning salt, paprika, and black pepper. Shake the bag to make sure everything is well incorporated. Start adding in the oxtails, one at a time, and shaking the bag to coat them. Once the oxtails are coated, set them on a plate or baking sheet.

- In a large pan over medium heat, pour in the vegetable oil. Once the oil is hot, start adding in the oxtails. Brown all surfaces of the oxtails, about 3 minutes on each side, then remove from the pan and place them into a 6-quart slow cooker.

- Toss the onion into the pan and cook until tender. Add to the slow cooker with the oxtails, along with the tomatoes, garlic, thyme, and bay leaves.

- In a large bowl, combine the tomato paste and beef broth, and mix until well combined. Pour this mixture into the slow cooker, set the slow cooker on low, and cook for 6 hours.

- Add the carrots and potatoes, stir, and cook for 2 more hours. Then serve and enjoy!

Beef Meatloaf

◇◇

When I first met my husband, I asked him what his favorite dish was. I assumed that he'd say steak or something else fancy or special. But it turns out he's just a laid-back meatloaf kind of guy—and I love him for that.

This means I've made a lot of meatloaf over the years! This is the version I've perfected over time. It's my go-to for busy weeknights because it's budget friendly and easy to whip together very quickly. But that doesn't mean you sacrifice any flavor, because this one has a secret ingredient: salsa! You'll want to serve it with some of my Cheesy Whipped Potatoes (page 91).

MAKES 8 TO 10 SERVINGS

Vegetable oil, for greasing	1 egg
5 slices white bread	2 teaspoons seasoning salt
½ cup whole milk	1 teaspoon garlic powder
2 pounds 80/20 ground beef	¼ to ½ cup ketchup, depending on
½ cup chunky mild salsa	how saucy you like it
¼ cup chopped green onions	

◆ Preheat the oven to 375 degrees F. Lightly grease a 9-by-13-inch baking dish.

◆ In a large mixing bowl, add the white bread and pour in the milk. Let the milk saturate the bread, then add in the ground beef, salsa, green onions, egg, seasoning salt, and garlic powder. Mix everything using your hands or a kitchen utensil until well combined.

◆ Mold the meatloaf into your desired shape and place it into the baking dish. Bake, uncovered, for 45 minutes.

◆ Remove the meatloaf from the oven, then slather the ketchup all over. Place it back into the oven, uncovered, for another 20 to 25 minutes, until the edges are browned. Let the meatloaf sit for 10 minutes before serving.

Baked Turkey Wings

My mom was always way better at buying turkey wings than she was at making them, so they'd sit around in our deep freezer until we were all out of chicken and one of us (usually me) had to give in and make something with them. Looking back, I'm wondering what we were thinking! Now, I love using turkey wings because they are so much bigger and have so much more flavor than chicken wings. I finally figured out the secret: I just season them lightly because they're already so good, then bake them in the oven until the meat literally starts to fall off the bone. The big flavors go well with Cornbread Dressing (page 119).

MAKES 6 SERVINGS

Vegetable oil, for greasing
2½ pounds turkey wings, flats and drums separated
1 large lemon, cut into 4 wedges
2 tablespoons extra-virgin olive oil or vegetable oil
1½ tablespoons plain or smoked paprika
1 tablespoon garlic powder
1 tablespoon onion powder
2 teaspoons dried parsley flakes
2 teaspoons poultry seasoning
2 teaspoons seasoning salt
1 teaspoon minced onion
1 teaspoon minced garlic
2½ cups turkey or chicken broth

- Preheat the oven to 350 degrees F. Lightly grease a 9-by-13-inch baking dish or an 8-quart Dutch oven.

- Clean the turkey wings, then rub the surfaces of the wings with the lemon wedges. Do not discard the wedges.

- In a large bowl or dish, add the wings and drizzle oil over them. Sprinkle the paprika, garlic and onion powders, parsley, poultry seasoning, salt, onion, and garlic all over the wings, and rub the seasonings in. Place the wings into the baking dish or Dutch oven.

- In the large bowl the wings were in, pour the broth over the leftover seasonings. Stir, then pour the broth into the baking dish with the wings. Add the lemon wedges.

- Cover the baking dish with aluminum foil or put the lid on the Dutch oven, and bake the wings in the oven for 1½ to 2 hours. Periodically remove the wings from the oven and baste with the drippings in the dish. Once done, remove from the oven and let cool before serving.

Southern Fried Chicken

FAN
FAVE!

I can pretty much thank fried chicken for this entire book: my very first video recipe on YouTube was a fried chicken video. And though my videos have improved since then, I have to say my fried chicken recipe was already perfect.

When making true Southern fried chicken, I believe less is better. You do not need ten herbs and seasonings, a complicated twenty-four-hour brine, or an egg mixture for this chicken. The secret to this chicken is the buttermilk soak—and you don't need any extra salt, because the buttermilk is already salty. And when you take it out of the soak, you don't need to rinse it at all, because that buttermilk is what will help the breading stick. This is some easygoing chicken, just let the buttermilk work its magic.

MAKES 4 SERVINGS

2 pounds chicken pieces, rinsed and trimmed of fat

4 to 6 cups buttermilk

1 teaspoon poultry seasoning

2 teaspoons kosher salt, divided

2 teaspoons garlic powder, divided

2 teaspoons onion powder, divided

1 teaspoon ground black pepper

1½ cups all-purpose flour

1 teaspoon smoked paprika

1 teaspoon ground white pepper

2 cups canola or corn oil, for deep-frying

◆ In a large bowl, combine the chicken and the buttermilk. Cover the bowl and place in the refrigerator for 3 to 4 hours. Then drain the buttermilk from the chicken, but do not rinse it.

◆ In the same bowl, season the chicken with the poultry seasoning, 1 teaspoon of the salt, 1 teaspoon of the garlic powder, 1 teaspoon of the onion powder, and the black pepper. Rub the seasonings all over the chicken, then set the bowl aside.

◆ In a separate large bowl, add the flour and the remaining seasonings: 1 teaspoon of salt, 1 teaspoon of garlic powder, 1 teaspoon of onion powder, paprika, and white pepper. Mix well. Coat the chicken with the seasoned flour two times.

◆ In a deep-frying pan or deep fryer, heat the oil to 360 degrees F and deep-fry the chicken for about 10 to 15 minutes, or until golden brown and there is no blood when you pierce a piece down to the bone. Remove the chicken pieces and let them sit for 5 minutes before serving.

Smothered Chicken

FAN FAVE!

◇◇◇

My mom would make smothered chicken with lots of gravy and onions at least once a week when I was growing up, cooking the meat until it fell right off the bone, then spooning it over rice. I could never get enough. On nice days, I'd eat my dinner outside, and the other kids on the block would always beg me to share this—which I never did. Now that I cook it myself, I do it on the stove top so that I can add milk to the gravy to make it even creamier. And I still don't want to share it with anyone! I serve it over rice, just like my mom did, and with a side dish of Turnip and Mustard Greens with Salt Pork (page 100).

MAKES 4 SERVINGS	
1½ cups all-purpose flour	1 pound chicken pieces, cleaned
1 tablespoon garlic powder	¼ cup vegetable oil
1 tablespoon onion powder	1 medium yellow onion, chopped
1 teaspoon kosher salt	2 teaspoons minced garlic
1 teaspoon ground black pepper	2 cups chicken broth
1 teaspoon celery seed	1 cup whole milk
1 teaspoon poultry seasoning	Chopped fresh parsley, for garnish
1 teaspoon smoked paprika	

◆ In a large bowl, combine the flour, garlic and onion powders, salt, black pepper, celery seed, poultry seasoning, and paprika. Mix until well incorporated.

◆ Coat the chicken with the seasoned flour, making sure you coat all surfaces. Reserve the remaining seasoned flour.

◆ In a large pan over medium heat, add the oil. Start adding in the chicken, but be sure not to overcrowd the pan (use a pan big enough to hold all of the chicken, or cook the chicken in batches). Cook the chicken until it is golden brown, about 7 minutes. Don't worry about cooking the chicken until it is done, because we will cook it some more later. Once the chicken is nicely browned, remove it from the pan and transfer to a plate covered with paper towels. Leave the oil in the pan.

◆ In the same pan, toss in the onions and cook for about 2 minutes. Add in the garlic and cook for an additional minute. Remove the onions and garlic from the pan and place in a bowl.

- Add 3 tablespoons of the remaining seasoned flour to the pan. Stir into the oil over medium heat. Pour in the chicken broth while whisking, and make sure there aren't any lumps. Let the gravy cook for about 2 minutes on medium heat, then pour the milk into the pan. Let the creamy gravy cook for about 3 minutes, then start adding the chicken, onions, and garlic back into the pan. Make sure all of the chicken is coated with gravy.

- Place a lid on the pan and cook the chicken for 30 to 35 minutes over medium heat. Be sure to occasionally turn the chicken. Once done, garnish with parsley and serve the chicken with rice or mashed potatoes.

Jerk Chicken

Caribbean food and soul food go hand in hand. If you go into a soul food restaurant, you'll sometimes see some Caribbean food on the menu as well. I don't know the whole history there, but my great-grandmother was from Jamaica, so the crossover between them has always been natural to me.

I knew my great-grandma pretty well, but she never cooked me any Jamaican food, which I thought was weird. So when I started cooking, I did a little research (mostly by eating at Jamaican restaurants!) and learned how to make some of my favorite Caribbean foods—like jerk chicken. Even though it didn't come from her, I still feel like it gives me some connection to my Jamaican heritage when I cook it. I love serving my jerk chicken with Red Beans and Rice (page 114) and Fried Cabbage (page 105).

MAKES 6 TO 8 SERVINGS

For the jerk marinade:
1 medium yellow onion, chopped
5 green onions, chopped, plus more for garnish
5 large whole garlic cloves
7 sprigs of fresh thyme, stemmed
3 tablespoons store-bought browning sauce
1 scotch bonnet pepper or jalapeño pepper if you want it more mild
Zest and juice from 1 small lime, plus sliced lime for garnish

2 tablespoons brown sugar
2 teaspoons kosher salt
2 teaspoons paprika
2 teaspoons ground allspice
1 teaspoon ground black pepper
½ teaspoon ground nutmeg
½ teaspoon grated fresh ginger

4 to 5 pounds chicken quarters, cleaned
Vegetable oil, for greasing

- In a blender or food processor, add all of the ingredients for the jerk marinade and blend until everything is well mixed.

- Toss the chicken into a large ziplock freezer bag, then pour in the marinade. Close the bag and move the chicken around to make sure it's well coated with the marinade. Let the chicken marinate in the refrigerator overnight or for a minimum of 6 hours.

- Once the chicken is good to go, preheat the oven to 375 degrees F. Place the chicken in a lightly oiled 9-by-13-inch baking dish. Bake in the oven, uncovered, for 1 hour and 15 minutes. Remove the chicken from the oven, and let cool. Garnish with lime and green onion before serving.

Dirty-Rice-Stuffed Cornish Hens

◇◇◇

Dirty rice is a dish that I grew up on. It's cheap to make, it's very filling, and it's full of Creole flavor and a bit of heat. But my mom would always make way too much at one time, so she found that stuffing it into these little birds managed to make it even better on the second day. The name "dirty rice" comes from the way the chicken livers and sausage color the rice, but it doesn't even matter what it looks like here, because it's inside that Cornish hen. This recipe is on the spicy side, so if you don't like it spicy, replace the hot sausage for mild and omit the red pepper flakes.

MAKES 4 SERVINGS

For the dirty rice
¼ pound chicken livers
2 teaspoons seasoning salt
1 teaspoon ground black pepper
½ pound ground hot Italian sausage
1 small green bell pepper, diced
1 large red onion, diced
1½ teaspoons Creole seasoning
½ teaspoon red pepper flakes

¼ cup chicken broth
4 cups cooked white rice

◇◇◇◇◇◇◇◇◇◇◇◇◇◇◇◇◇◇◇◇◇◇◇◇◇◇◇◇◇

2 Cornish hens, cavities emptied
2 tablespoons vegetable oil
2½ teaspoons seasoning salt
2 teaspoons paprika
1 teaspoon poultry seasoning
1 teaspoon ground black pepper
Butter, for greasing

◆ In a medium bowl, season the chicken livers with seasoning salt and black pepper. Set to the side.

◆ In a large pan over medium heat, cook the sausage until browned, then remove from the pan and set aside. Toss the chicken livers into the pan and cook for about 10 minutes or so, or until done, then remove from the pan. Set aside the livers with the sausage.

◆ In the same pan still over medium heat, cook the peppers and onions until they soften. Dice up the chicken livers, then add them back to the pan along with the sausage. Sprinkle in the Creole seasoning and red pepper flakes, then pour in the chicken broth. Stir the ingredients and add the rice. Cook for 5 minutes, then turn off the heat and set the rice to the side to cool slightly.

◆ Preheat the oven to 375 degrees F. Place the Cornish hens on a baking sheet and drizzle the oil all over them. Season the hens with the seasoning salt, paprika, poultry seasoning, and black pepper. Rub the seasonings in, then start stuffing the Cornish hens with the dirty rice. (There will be dirty rice left over.)

◆ Lightly butter a 9-by-13-inch baking dish. Put the remaining dirty rice in the baking dish, then put the stuffed Cornish hens (breast down) on top. Place the baking dish in the oven and cook for 50 to 55 minutes. Remove from the oven, and let cool for 10 minutes. Cut lengthwise to serve, and enjoy!

Cajun Fried Shrimp and Oysters

◇◇◇

Oysters have a special place in my heart because they are deeply rooted in my family's home in Louisiana and my own home of Washington State. Lots of people have opinions about which state has better oysters, but for me, I just say, if it's an oyster, I'm going to eat it!

These oysters and shrimp get cooked Louisiana style, though—dredged in Cajun seasoning and cornmeal and dropped right into the deep fryer. Since you've already got the oil going, you might as well make their classic pairing from Cajun country, Hush Puppies (page 124), to go with them.

MAKES 4 SERVINGS

1 pound fresh shucked oysters	½ cup yellow cornmeal
1 pound jumbo raw shrimp, peeled and deveined	2 teaspoons Cajun seasoning
2 eggs, lightly beaten separately	½ teaspoon lemon pepper
¾ cup all-purpose flour	2 cups vegetable oil, for deep-frying

---

◆ Place the oysters in a medium bowl, and place the shrimp in a separate bowl. Drizzle the eggs over the shrimp and oysters (1 egg per bowl) and make sure everything is nicely coated. Set the bowls to the side.

◆ In a large ziplock freezer bag, add the flour, cornmeal, Cajun seasoning, and lemon pepper. Shake up the bag to make sure everything is well mixed. Add the shrimp to the bag and shake to coat, then remove the shrimp and place them on a baking sheet. Now add the oysters to the bag and repeat the process.

◆ In a deep fryer or deep-frying pan, heat the vegetable oil to about 350 to 360 degrees F. Fry the shrimp until it's golden brown, approximately 3 to 4 minutes. Then fry the oysters until golden brown, approximately 5 minutes. Place the seafood on a paper-towel-lined plate to help absorb some of the excess oil. Serve with your favorite dipping sauce.

Smoked Salmon

My grandpa and I were super close; I would sit with him and listen to stories about my grandma, the Southern belle, for hours. Smoked salmon was one of his favorite foods. He'd always buy it from the store, and he would only ever share a tiny pinch with me because he was greedy! But, honestly, I wouldn't want to share my smoked salmon with anyone either if I had to buy it or make it the usual way in a smoker, which takes forever. Since I use this super-simple oven-smoked method, it's easy to make enough for everyone, and y'all can even share it with your grandchildren (if you want to).

MAKES 6 SERVINGS

2 tablespoons dark brown sugar
1 tablespoon granulated sugar
1 tablespoon onion powder
1 tablespoon garlic powder
1 teaspoon kosher salt
1 teaspoon coarse black pepper

½ teaspoon red pepper flakes
2 pounds salmon fillets, boneless
  and skinless
2 tablespoons liquid smoke
Vegetable oil, for greasing
Lemon wedges, for serving

---

* In a large ziplock bag, add the sugars, onion and garlic powders, salt, black pepper, and red pepper flakes. Close the bag, then shake to make sure everything is well combined. Toss in the salmon fillets, and drizzle in the liquid smoke. Close the bag and shake to make sure the salmon is well coated. Place the bag in the refrigerator for 8 hours.

* Preheat the oven to 350 degrees F. Lightly grease a 9-by-13-inch baking dish lined with parchment paper.

* Take the bag from the refrigerator, remove the salmon, and place it in the dish. Discard the bag. Bake the salmon, uncovered, for 20 to 25 minutes. Remove from the oven, and let it cool. Serve with lemon.

Deep-Fried Catfish

At least once on every family trip to Baton Rouge, someone hosts a fish fry in their backyard. All the kids run around playing while the older aunts and grand-mas crowd around a deep fryer. The easy Motown music plays from an old stereo, and there's a table all set out full of cornbread, potato salad, hush puppies, corn on the cob with spray-on butter, and big containers of sweet tea. When the kids finally sit down at the table, someone will usually bring over a bucket of whole crab for them to gnaw on, but nobody brings over the catfish—when we wanted some of that as kids, we had to get on up and grab our own! It never lasted long enough for anyone to bring it over. Now I make my own version, and it's still so good it barely makes it to the table.

To help the seasoned cornmeal and flour really stick to the fish, I like to coat the catfish with yellow mustard. Don't worry: you won't taste the mustard, unless you have super-sensitive taste buds.

MAKES 4 SERVINGS

2 pounds catfish fillets
¼ cup yellow mustard
1 cup yellow cornmeal
¾ cup self-rising flour
2¾ teaspoons seasoning salt
1½ teaspoons paprika

1 teaspoon ground black pepper
2 cups vegetable oil, for deep-frying
Tartar sauce and lemon wedges,
    for serving
Chopped fresh parsley, for garnish

◆ Coat the catfish with the yellow mustard and place them on a baking sheet. Set to the side.

◆ In a large ziplock freezer bag, add the cornmeal, self-rising flour, seasoning salt, paprika, and black pepper. Shake the bag to make sure everything is well combined, then start adding in the catfish. Make sure the catfish is nicely coated, then remove the fillets from the bag and place them on a plate.

◆ Heat up the oil in your deep fryer or deep-frying pan to 350 to 360 degrees F, then deep-fry the catfish until it's nice and golden brown (usually 10 minutes, but could be a few minutes longer if the fish is thick). If you're using a deep-frying pan, turn the fish every 3 to 5 minutes. Remove the fish from the oil and set it on a paper-towel-lined plate to help absorb the excess oil. Serve with tartar sauce and lemon wedges, and garnish with parsley.

Shrimp Étouffée

This dish is just about as Louisiana as they get. You know how much I love a smothered dish? Well, *étouffée* just means "smothered" in French, which is what Cajun people used to speak.

The only trick to this dish is the roux, which takes a little bit of patience and babysitting. Don't leave the kitchen when you're cooking a roux, because somehow a roux can sense those things, and it will burn the minute you turn around. Once it burns, there's no going back: you have to start over. But when you do it right, the roux will also be what thickens your sauce and gives it a great flavor.

MAKES 4 SERVINGS

½ cup (1 stick) salted butter
½ cup all-purpose flour
1 tablespoon vegetable oil
1 large green bell pepper, diced
½ medium onion, diced
2 stalks celery, diced
3 garlic cloves, minced
1 (14-ounce) can diced tomatoes
1 tablespoon tomato paste
2 cups chicken broth or seafood stock

2 sprigs of fresh thyme, plus more
   for garnish
1½ teaspoons Creole seasoning
1 teaspoon Worcestershire sauce
½ teaspoon ground black pepper
½ teaspoon red pepper flakes
2 pounds raw jumbo shrimp, peeled
   and deveined
2 cups cooked white rice

◆ In a large saucepan over medium heat, melt the butter. Once the butter is melted, add in the flour and whisk until everything is well combined. Cook the roux until it reaches a nice, rich brown color, 10 to 15 minutes, but be sure not to burn it!

◆ Add in the bell peppers, onions, celery, and garlic. Cook until the veggies soften, 3 to 5 minutes. Then add the diced tomatoes and tomato paste. Slowly pour in the broth and toss in the fresh thyme. Mix until everything is well combined, then sprinkle in the Creole seasoning, Worcestershire sauce, black pepper, and red pepper flakes. Stir the ingredients, and let cook for 5 minutes over medium-high heat.

◆ Slowly start adding in the shrimp, and stir. Reduce the heat to low and cook for 5 more minutes. Remove the thyme sprigs. Garnish with thyme and serve with hot rice.

Gumbo

◇◇

Gumbo is something of a sacred tradition among Louisiana folk—it's basically just a big ol' pot of seafood. Just don't try to call it a stew—you'll make the Creole people in my family real mad.

This gumbo is what's called a red gumbo because of the tomatoes and because it uses a slightly lighter roux than a brown one would. But I also make a few of my own tweaks. I'm sick of picking out the bones, so instead of the traditional wings, I use boneless, skinless chicken thighs for the meat. And the true secret to my gumbo, passed down from my grandma, is adding dried shrimp to really boost that seafood flavor. You can usually find dried shrimp in Asian markets. I like to serve my gumbo with rice and Sweet Cornbread (page 122).

MAKES 8 TO 10 SERVINGS

1¼ cup vegetable oil, divided

1 pound boneless, skinless
   chicken thighs

2 teaspoons seasoning salt, divided

1½ teaspoons ground black pepper,
   divided

1 teaspoon poultry seasoning

1 teaspoon onion powder

1 teaspoon garlic powder

2 quarts chicken broth, divided

1½ cups chopped celery

2 large green bell peppers, chopped

1 large yellow onion, chopped

2 teaspoons minced garlic

½ cup all-purpose flour

1 pound andouille sausage, chopped

1 (14-ounce) can diced tomatoes

3 to 4 bay leaves

½ pound okra, chopped

1 cup dried shrimp

2 pounds Alaskan king crab

1 pound large shrimp, peeled and
   deveined

2½ teaspoons ground gumbo filé

Chopped fresh parsley, for garnish

◆ In a medium skillet over medium heat, pour in ¼ cup of the vegetable oil. Once the oil is hot, place the chicken thighs in the skillet. Season the chicken with 1 teaspoon of the seasoning salt, ½ teaspoon of the black pepper, the poultry seasoning, onion powder, and garlic powder. Brown each side of the chicken, about 5 minutes per side, then pour in ½ cup of the chicken broth. Cover the skillet and let the chicken cook until it is completely cooked through, about 15 minutes. Once done, remove the chicken from the skillet and set to the side on a plate.

CONTINUED

- In the same skillet, add the celery, bell peppers, and onions, and cook for 2 minutes. Add the garlic, and cook until the veggies are nice and translucent, then turn the heat off.

- In a large stockpot over medium heat, pour in the remaining 1 cup vegetable oil. Once the oil is hot, start sprinkling in the flour just a little bit at a time. Stir continuously to prevent lumps and cook until the roux turns into a peanut butter–brown color, about 30 minutes.

- Once the roux is nice and brown, slowly pour in the remaining chicken broth. Add in the cooked vegetables, chicken, and sausage. Give everything a nice stir, and sprinkle in the remaining 1 teaspoon seasoning salt and 1 teaspoon black pepper. Add the tomatoes and bay leaves. Stir, cover, then cook for about 20 minutes.

- Add in the chopped okra and dried shrimp. Stir, cover, and simmer for 20 more minutes.

- Now add the crab. Make sure that the crab and other ingredients are nicely covered with the broth. Simmer for another 20 minutes, then toss in the raw shrimp. Stir the ingredients and reduce the heat to low.

- Sprinkle in the gumbo filé, stir, and cook for 7 minutes. Turn the heat off and let the gumbo sit for a couple of minutes. Garnish with parsley, and serve with steamed rice or cornbread.

What Is a Roux?

When I make gumbo or shrimp étouffée, or any number of other dishes, you'll notice that I often refer to a roux. The roux is an important part of these and so many soul food dishes because it adds a ton of flavor and also helps thicken the dish to the right texture. The ingredients for a roux are simple: just butter or oil, flour, and an almost infinite amount of patience. See, you have to keep stirring the roux as it browns to make it come together. For a simple gravy, like the one that goes with my Chicken Fried Steak (page 39), that might be just a few minutes. But for my Gumbo (page 175), you're looking at half an hour—and that's nothing compared to some people's! And you really do have to babysit it and stir the whole time so that the heat slowly builds in that nutty flavor without burning it—if you burn your roux, you've got to toss it and start over again. Best just to keep an eye on it the whole time!

Salmon Croquettes

FAN FAVE!

◇◇◇

These simple little patties are a great way to use up leftover salmon, or you can use canned salmon. When I was growing up, we ate a lot of canned salmon because it was very cheap.

You can serve these for dinner with some tartar sauce and my Soul Food Macaroni and Cheese (page 87)—but they also work great as breakfast with grits and eggs or, for lunch, just stick them on buns and call it a salmon burger.

MAKES 6 SERVINGS

1 (14.75-ounce) can salmon, drained, or 1½ cups leftover salmon

1 small onion, diced

1 egg

½ cup plain dried bread crumbs

1½ teaspoons garlic powder

1 teaspoon seasoning salt

1 teaspoon lemon juice

½ teaspoon ground black pepper

½ cup vegetable oil

◆ In a large mixing bowl, combine the salmon, onions, egg, bread crumbs, garlic powder, seasoning salt, lemon juice, and black pepper. Mix the ingredients until everything is well incorporated. Form the salmon mixture into patties, then set to the side.

◆ In a large skillet over medium heat, pour in the oil. Once the oil is hot, add in a few patties and fry for about 5 minutes on each side until nice and golden. Serve and enjoy for breakfast, lunch, or dinner!

Seafood-Stuffed Peppers

This is one of the first meals I learned to make when I took over the family kitchen at age twelve. My mom had started working evening shifts, leaving me with the responsibility to make sure my little brother and I got our homework done and ate dinner. That means these are quick and easy enough for a tween to make—but they are also good enough that everyone will want to eat them. They'll be plenty moist, so they don't need a sauce or anything, and with a bit of salad on the side, this can be a full meal.

MAKES 6 SERVINGS

2 tablespoons vegetable oil, plus more for greasing

3 large green bell peppers, halved lengthwise and seeds removed

6 ounces store-bought cornbread dressing mix, unseasoned

⅔ cup chopped green onions

½ cup crab meat, cooked

½ cup shrimp meat, cooked

1 egg

1½ teaspoons Creole seasoning

1 teaspoon minced garlic

4 tablespoons salted butter, melted

2 cups seafood or chicken stock

+ Preheat the oven to 350 degrees F. Lightly oil a 9-by-13-inch baking dish and place the bell peppers facedown in the dish. Drizzle the oil over the peppers, place the baking dish in the oven, and cook until they are slightly brown. Remove the peppers from the oven and set to the side.

+ In a large bowl, combine the dressing mix, green onions, crab, shrimp, egg, Creole seasoning, and garlic. Mix until everything is well combined, then add in the melted butter and stock. Stir the mixture, then let sit for 10 minutes so that the cornbread dressing mix can absorb all the flavors.

+ Arrange the peppers faceup in the baking dish and stuff them with the seafood dressing mixture. Place the peppers in the oven and cook for 30 to 35 minutes. Let cool before serving.

Crab, Shrimp, and Lobster Pot Pie

◇◇◇

I just love a good old-fashioned chicken pot pie, especially during the colder months. Honestly, I love all types of pot pie—even the little frozen ones, no shame in my game. Still, nothing screams comfort food like the steam rising out of a homemade pot pie as it comes out of the oven. But you know I'm a seafood girl, so I had to try it—and it works great. It's almost like a chowder inside the pie with how creamy it is.

MAKES 6 SERVINGS

3 tablespoons extra-virgin olive oil	1 cup whole milk
2 medium red potatoes, peeled and diced	1 cup lump crab meat
½ medium red onion, diced	1 cup lobster meat
1½ cups frozen peas and carrots, thawed	1 cup (or half pound) medium raw shrimp, peeled and deveined
½ cup salted butter	2½ teaspoons Creole seasoning
½ cup all-purpose flour	2 refrigerated store-bought pie crusts
1½ cups seafood stock	1 egg, beaten
	1 tablespoon water

- Preheat oven to 425 degrees F.

- In a medium pan over medium heat, add the oil. Once the oil is hot, toss in the potatoes, and cook until tender. Add the onions and cook for 5 minutes before adding in the peas and carrots. Cook for 3 more minutes, then turn off the heat, and set to the side.

- In a large saucepan over medium heat, melt the butter, then sprinkle in the flour. Cook for about 3 to 4 minutes. Whisk in the seafood stock and milk. Add the vegetables, seafood, and Creole seasoning, and stir gently.

- Place 1 pie crust into the bottom of a deep-dish pie pan, then pour the seafood filling into the pie shell. Place second pie crust on top of the seafood mixture, and pinch the sides of the crust to seal.

- In a small bowl, mix the beaten egg and water, then brush the top of the pot pie with the mixture. Bake the pot pie for 30 minutes, uncovered. Cool slightly before serving.

Jambalaya-Stuffed Cabbage Rolls

I know what you're thinking, *Jambalaya-Stuffed Cabbage Rolls?!* Yes! I went there! I love jambalaya and stuffed cabbage rolls, so I decided to combine the two. I make an easy jambalaya with shrimp and smoked sausage, then I roll it in cabbage leaves, smother the cabbage in a red sauce, and bake it. It's a bit extra, but so am I sometimes!

MAKES 6 TO 8 SERVINGS

2 tablespoons extra-virgin olive oil

1 pound andouille sausage, chopped

1 large red bell pepper, diced

1 large green bell pepper, diced

1 large red onion, chopped

1 (14.5-ounce) can diced tomatoes, undrained

2 tablespoons tomato paste

5 garlic cloves, minced

2½ teaspoons Cajun seasoning, divided

2 teaspoons dried thyme

2 teaspoons paprika

2 teaspoons Worcestershire sauce

1½ teaspoons celery salt

3 bay leaves

6 cups vegetable broth, divided

1½ cups uncooked white rice

1 pound medium raw shrimp, peeled and deveined

1 large head of cabbage, leaves individually removed

Vegetable oil, for greasing

1 cup canned tomato sauce

Kosher salt and black pepper, to taste

◆ In a large stockpot over medium heat, drizzle the oil. Once the oil is hot, toss in the sausage and cook until it browns. Remove the sausage from the pot and set it to the side.

◆ Next, add the peppers and onions. Cook until they are nice and tender, then add in the tomatoes (with the juice), tomato paste, and garlic. Stir well. Add in 2 teaspoons of the Cajun seasoning, the thyme, paprika, Worcestershire sauce, celery salt, bay leaves, and 3 cups of the vegetable broth. Stir the ingredients, then add the sausage back into the pot, along with the uncooked rice. Stir again and cook for 25 to 30 minutes, or until the liquid is absorbed. Then add the shrimp, stir, and remove from the heat. Set to the side.

◆ In a separate stockpot over medium heat, add the cabbage leaves and the remaining 3 cups vegetable broth. Cook until the cabbage softens, then drain and cool.

- Lightly oil a baking dish. Wrap about ¼ cup jambalaya in each cabbage leaf and place the rolls in the baking dish. Set to the side.

- In a small bowl, combine the tomato sauce, the remaining ½ teaspoon Cajun seasoning, salt, and pepper. Stir until well combined.

- Pour the tomato sauce all over the cabbage rolls, then cover the baking dish with aluminum foil and bake in the oven for 25 to 30 minutes. Remove from the oven and let cool before serving.

Baked Spaghetti

Baked spaghetti is kind of like a lazy person's lasagna—and it was the only way we had spaghetti when I was growing up. I used to sit right in front of the oven while it baked and watch the cheese get all nice and bubbly on top. Now, I make it all the time for big groups because it's so easy—and because I can always have one ready to go in the freezer.

Freezing this easy baked spaghetti is simple—make it in an aluminum baking dish with a lid, and just before it would go in the oven, put the lid on and freeze it. When you're ready to cook it, simply remove from the freezer, let thaw, uncover, and bake for 30 to 40 minutes.

MAKES 10 TO 12 SERVINGS

2 pounds ground beef

1 pound ground Italian sausage

1 medium yellow onion, chopped

5 garlic cloves, minced

1 (45-ounce) jar of chunky pasta
    sauce

1 tablespoon Italian seasoning

Kosher salt and black pepper, to taste

1 pound uncooked spaghetti

12 ounces yellow sharp cheddar
    cheese, shredded

6 ounces white sharp cheddar
    cheese, shredded

- In a large sauté pan over medium heat, brown the ground beef and sausage. Drain the fat, then toss in the onions and cook until translucent, 3 to 5 minutes. Add the garlic, pasta sauce, Italian seasoning, salt, and pepper. Stir the ingredients and turn the heat down to low. Cook for 10 minutes.

- While the sauce is simmering, cook the spaghetti pasta until al dente. Drain the pasta, then set to the side.

- Preheat the oven to 350 degrees F.

- In a 9-by-13-inch baking dish, add one-third of the meat sauce at the bottom. Next add half of the spaghetti pasta, then the sauce, followed by half of each of the cheeses. Repeat the layering process, ending with the cheese. Leave the spaghetti uncovered and bake for 30 to 40 minutes. Cool slightly before serving.

The Dessert Table

Peach Cobbler

My aunt Josie was—and still is—the Peach Cobbler Queen. Hers was the best recipe ever, and I wanted it so bad. But it doesn't matter how nice people are, Josie isn't giving that recipe away to anyone. She'll pretend she forgot it. She'll wave me away and say, "Oh, I use a little of this and some of that." She's a lovely person—when I was pregnant with my son, all I wanted in the world was her peach cobbler, and I appreciate that she was kind enough to bring one over to me, but she still would not give up that recipe. Well, I tasted the one she brought me, and I knew with my pregnancy cravings that I'd need more than that. I got straight to work trying to do my best impression of it—tasting hers and testing mine until they matched. She might be the queen, but maybe I can be the Peach Cobbler Princess.

MAKES 8 TO 10 SERVINGS

Vegetable oil, for greasing	½ cup (1 stick) salted butter
¼ cup all-purpose flour	1 tablespoon vanilla extract
½ cup water	1½ teaspoons ground cinnamon
2 (14.5-ounce) cans sliced peaches in heavy syrup	½ teaspoon ground ginger
	¼ teaspoon ground nutmeg
¾ cup granulated sugar	2 refrigerated store-bought pie crusts

---

◆ Preheat the oven to 350 degrees F. Lightly grease an 8-by-11-inch baking dish or oval baking dish.

◆ In a liquid measuring cup, add the flour and water, and mix. Set to the side.

◆ In a medium saucepan over medium-high heat, add the peaches, sugar, butter, vanilla, cinnamon, ginger, and nutmeg. Stir the ingredients and let the butter melt completely. Next, pour in the water-and-flour mixture. Stir and cook for 5 more minutes.

CONTINUED

- Roll out one of the pie doughs and cut into 2-inch squares. Put the squares into the baking dish, then pour in the cobbler filling. Roll out the second pie dough. Top the cobbler with the remaining dough.

- Brush any leftover cobbler filling from the pot on top of the cobbler. Bake the cobbler for 35 to 40 minutes. Cool slightly before serving.

Note: This cobbler has "dumplings." If you like the dumplings crisp, bake the dough squares (at 350 degrees F) for 5 to 7 minutes after rolling out and cutting them, then add them to the baking dish.

Liquid Measuring Cup versus Dry Measuring Cup

When cooking and baking, it's crucial to have both liquid and dry measuring cups. Depending on which cup you use to measure, you could end up with a different amount—you could possibly mess up a recipe if you use the wrong measuring cups, especially when it comes to baking.

With liquid measurements, you want to use a cup that has extra room so that if you pour in too much, it doesn't spill, and you can pour off any excess through the spout. For dry measurements, you're likely to scoop them out of a container, so they fit the exact cup size—then after you scoop, you can brush any excess back into the container with a flat utensil so that you have the exact right amount. These help you get the precise amount called for in the recipe so it turns out just like it should.

Red Velvet Cake

 FAN FAVE!

$\diamond$

A lot of people out there hate red velvet cake. They are wrong.

Maybe they've had some other, dried-out, poorly made cake, but my version uses buttermilk and vegetable oil so that it stays super moist the whole time it cooks. It's light and fluffy, and I like to use absurd amounts of red food coloring so that it looks as bright as it tastes.

I encourage you to alter the color to your preference, but don't change anything else. As you're making it, know that the batter will seem very thin—don't worry, that's part of how it stays moist. Trust me, and you'll end up with a vibrant cake that converts all the haters.

MAKES 10 TO 12 SERVINGS

2½ cups all-purpose flour	1 teaspoon distilled white vinegar
2 teaspoons unsweetened cocoa powder	1 ounce red food coloring
1 teaspoon kosher salt	**For the frosting:**
1 teaspoon baking soda	16 ounces cream cheese, softened
2 eggs, at room temperature	1 cup (2 sticks) unsalted butter, softened
1½ cups granulated sugar	8 cups powdered sugar
1½ cups vegetable oil	1 tablespoon whole milk
1 cup buttermilk, at room temperature	2 teaspoons vanilla extract
1½ teaspoons vanilla extract	

◆ Preheat the oven to 325 degrees F. Spray two 9-inch cake pans with baking spray, or grease and flour them.

◆ In a large mixing bowl, combine the flour, cocoa powder, salt, and baking soda and sift or whisk together.

◆ In a medium bowl, crack open the eggs and beat them with a whisk. Pour the sugar, oil, buttermilk, and vanilla into the bowl, and mix using a handheld mixer on low speed until everything is nice and creamy.

CONTINUED

- Slowly combine the wet ingredients with the dry ingredients in the large bowl. Be sure to mix on a low speed! Once everything is just combined, switch from mixing the cake batter with the handheld mixer to folding it using a spatula. Next, add the vinegar and red food coloring. Fold until all of the cake batter is red and there are no streaks.

- Pour an equal amount of cake batter into each cake pan. Shake and tap the pans to release any air bubbles, then let sit for 5 minutes. Bake the cakes for 25 to 30 minutes. Remove the cakes from the cake pans and place them on cooling racks.

- While the cakes are cooling, make the frosting. In a large bowl, combine the cream cheese and butter. Cream the two ingredients together using a handheld mixer, then slowly add in the powdered sugar 1 cup at a time. Add in the milk and vanilla, and mix until the frosting is nice and creamy. Once the cakes are completely cool, frost them.

Bread Pudding with Rum Sauce

◇◇

It wasn't until a subscriber asked for a bread pudding recipe that I realized I hadn't posted one. Well, as someone that comes from Louisiana people, where bread pudding is a staple, that just wasn't right. I went straight to work making my own recipe with plenty of cinnamon, nutmeg, and brown sugar. My favorite part of this is how soft and gooey the bread gets, so it's important that you use day-old bread because it will be dried out and then will absorb the custard better. And you have to let it soak for the full twenty-five minutes so that the custard seeps into every part of it before it bakes.

MAKES 8 TO 10 SERVINGS

Vegetable oil, for greasing
3 cups half-and-half
½ cup granulated sugar
½ cup brown sugar
5 eggs, lightly beaten
1 tablespoon vanilla extract
1½ teaspoons ground cinnamon
½ teaspoon ground nutmeg

1 (16-ounce) loaf day-old French
   bread, cubed

For the rum sauce:
1 cup heavy cream
4 tablespoons unsalted butter
½ cup powdered sugar
1 tablespoon all-purpose flour
2 teaspoons rum extract

◆ Preheat the oven to 350 degrees F. Lightly grease a 9-by-13-inch baking dish.

◆ In a large mixing bowl, combine the half-and-half, sugars, eggs, vanilla, cinnamon, and nutmeg, and mix until well combined, then set to the side.

◆ In the prepared dish, spread out the cubed bread evenly, pour the egg mixture over the bread, and let it sit for about 25 minutes. Bake in the oven, uncovered, for 45 to 50 minutes. Remove from the oven, then let cool.

◆ To make the sauce, pour the heavy cream into a large saucepan over medium heat. Add the butter, powdered sugar, and flour. Cook for about 5 minutes, or until the sauce thickens. Add in the rum extract, then turn off the heat. Stir, then spoon the sauce over the bread pudding. Serve and enjoy!

Mixed Berry Cobbler with Sugar Biscuits

Because in my family we never have just one dessert, I always notice that so many pies all look the same. We eat with our eyes first, and if all you see is plain crust on top of every pie, well, that gets old pretty fast. So when I have people coming over, instead of using a pie crust, I top my mixed berry cobbler with a homemade sugar-biscuit topping to give it a special look—just what a special dessert like this deserves.

This version is also definitely for guests because I'm actually allergic to strawberries! If I make it for myself, I'll just double one of the other berries.

MAKES 10 SERVINGS

Vegetable oil, for greasing
2 cups fresh strawberries, sliced
2 cups fresh blackberries
2 cups fresh blueberries
1 cup granulated sugar
¾ cup water
2 tablespoons unsalted butter
1 tablespoon vanilla extract
3 tablespoons cornstarch

For the biscuit topping:
2 cups all-purpose flour
¼ cup granulated sugar
3 tablespoons baking powder
½ teaspoon kosher salt
¾ cup buttermilk
5 tablespoons cold unsalted butter, shredded
2 teaspoons vanilla extract
2 tablespoons melted unsalted butter
2 tablespoons coarse sugar

♦ Preheat the oven to 375 degrees F. Lightly grease a 9-by-13-inch baking dish.

♦ In a large pot over medium heat, combine the berries with the sugar, water, butter, and vanilla. When bubbles start to form, scoop out about ¼ cup liquid from the pot.

♦ In a small bowl, combine the ¼ cup of hot liquid with the cornstarch and mix until lump-free. Pour the cornstarch mixture back into the pot with the berries and stir. Cook until everything thickens, then pour the fruit mixture into the baking dish. Set aside.

For the biscuit topping, in a large bowl, combine the flour, sugar, baking powder, and salt. Whisk until well combined. Add in the buttermilk, shredded butter, and vanilla. Mix the ingredients. Scoop out the biscuit mixture and place it on top of the berry filling.

Brush the biscuits with melted butter, then sprinkle on the coarse sugar. Bake in the oven, uncovered, for 30 to 35 minutes. Remove from the oven, and let cool. Serve with or without ice cream.

Easy Lemon Bars

Forget chocolate bunnies, I looked forward to Easter because it was the one time of year my mom would make us lemon bars. She wasn't a big baker, so pretty soon I realized that if I wanted them any more often, I was going to have to make them myself.

The most important thing for this recipe is to use fresh lemons so that you can scrape off the zest and then squeeze out the juice. You want the filling to be perfectly smooth and thick before you pour it in, and that shortbread crust on the bottom should be nice and crumbly.

MAKES 12 SERVINGS

For the shortbread:
1¾ cups all-purpose flour
½ cup granulated sugar
¼ cup cornstarch
½ teaspoon ground nutmeg
¼ teaspoon kosher salt
1 cup (2 sticks) unsalted butter, softened

For the filling:
1½ cups granulated sugar
¼ cup all-purpose flour
4 eggs, lightly beaten
½ cup freshly squeezed lemon juice (from about 3 large lemons)
2 teaspoons lemon zest
Powdered sugar, for dusting

◆ Preheat the oven to 350 degrees F. Line a 9-by-13-inch baking pan with parchment paper, and spray with nonstick cooking spray.

◆ In a large mixing bowl, whisk together the flour, sugar, cornstarch, nutmeg, and salt. Add the butter to the flour mixture, and mix using a fork until it's crumbly.

◆ Place the mixture into the prepared baking pan and press it down into an even layer. Bake the shortbread base for 20 to 25 minutes, or until it slightly browns. Remove from the oven and set aside.

◆ To make the lemon filling, in a large mixing bowl, whisk the sugar and flour until well combined. Add the eggs, lemon juice, and lemon zest, and mix thoroughly. Pour the lemon filling over the shortbread.

◆ Bake for 20 to 22 minutes, until the lemon filling is set. Remove from the oven and let cool to room temperature before placing in the refrigerator for 2 hours. Sift a little powdered sugar on top before serving.

Egg Custard Bars

<><><><><><><><><><><><><><><><><><><><><><><><><><><><><><><><><><>

Custard is one of my favorite desserts, but when I want to fancy it up for the holidays, I get to work on my egg custard bars. They are super rich, with eggs, sugar, and evaporated milk, and the crust is made out of vanilla wafers—which might remind you a bit of banana pudding. You can also make them with graham crackers instead, for a slightly warmer flavor.

MAKES 12 SERVINGS

For the crust:
Vegetable oil, for greasing
1 package of crushed vanilla wafers
1 cup (2 sticks) unsalted butter, softened
¾ cup granulated sugar

For the custard:
4 cups evaporated milk, divided
6 eggs, lightly beaten
⅔ cup granulated sugar
2 tablespoons all-purpose flour
1 teaspoon vanilla extract
¼ teaspoon ground nutmeg

◆ Preheat the oven to 325 degrees F. Lightly grease a 9-by-13-inch baking dish.

◆ In a large bowl, add the crushed vanilla wafers, butter, and sugar. Mix the ingredients until they are well combined and resemble wet sand.

◆ Sprinkle the vanilla wafer mixture into the baking dish, pressing evenly into the bottom of the dish. Set to the side.

◆ In a large saucepan over medium heat, warm 3 cups of the evaporated milk. Cook until bubbles form, then turn off the heat.

◆ In a medium mixing bowl, combine the remaining 1 cup evaporated milk with the eggs, sugar, flour, vanilla, and nutmeg. Mix until well combined. Slowly pour the egg mixture into the saucepan with the hot milk. Whisk thoroughly.

◆ Pour the custard mixture into the baking dish, over the vanilla wafer crust. Bake in the oven for 45 to 50 minutes, or until the custard is firm. Remove from the oven and let cool before serving.

Sweet Potato Pie

Sweet potato pie is probably one of the most common soul food desserts. My aunt Nisha always made the one for our dessert table, but for mine I do a few things differently. First, in the crust I add a little bit of vanilla so that it matches the flavor of the filling. I also use real butter for flavor, but also a little bit of butter-flavored shortening for texture. For the filling, I use evaporated milk, again for texture, but my real secret ingredient is for the flavor: ground ginger. It adds a ton of warmth and plays so nicely with the vanilla. But if you are not a fan of ginger, you can leave it out.

MAKES 10 TO 12 SERVINGS

For the crust:
Vegetable oil, for greasing
1¼ cups all-purpose flour
¼ cup cold salted butter, diced or shredded
¼ cup butter-flavored shortening
2 tablespoons granulated sugar
1 teaspoon vanilla extract
½ teaspoon kosher salt
1½ tablespoons ice water

For the filling:
3 medium sweet potatoes, peeled and chopped
1 cup granulated sugar
1 teaspoon ground cinnamon
½ teaspoon ground nutmeg
¼ teaspoon ground ginger
2 eggs
½ cup evaporated milk
1 tablespoon vanilla extract
1 cup (2 sticks) salted butter, softened

◆ Preheat the oven to 325 degrees F. Lightly grease a 9-inch pie pan.

◆ In a large mixing bowl, combine the flour, butter, shortening, sugar, vanilla, salt, and ice water. Mix the ingredients until a dough forms, then wrap with plastic wrap and store the dough in the refrigerator for 1 to 2 hours.

◆ In a medium pot over high heat, add the sweet potatoes and about 4 to 6 cups of water. Boil the potatoes until they are fork-tender. Once the potatoes are done, drain the water and let the potatoes cool.

◆ Toss the cooled sweet potatoes into a large mixing bowl, and whisk until the potatoes are nice and creamy. Sprinkle in the sugar, cinnamon, nutmeg, and ginger. Mix the ingredients. Next, add the eggs, evaporated milk, vanilla, and butter. Whisk until the mixture is creamy and airy. Set the bowl to the side.

- Remove the dough from the refrigerator, flour a flat surface, and roll out the dough. Place it into the pie pan and bake the pie shell for 7 to 10 minutes.

- Remove the shell from the oven, then turn the heat up to 350 degrees F. Add the sweet potato filling to the pie shell and smooth it out. Bake the pie for 45 to 50 minutes, until the filling is set. Let the pie cool to room temperature before serving.

Old-Fashioned Buttermilk Pie

FAN FAVE!

If you've ever had a chess pie, you'll get the basic idea of this pie—it's kind of the lesser-known little sister that deserves a chance to shine. They both have a creamy, custardy filling, but the lemon juice and buttermilk in this give it a bit more of an exciting tang, and the vanilla really rounds out the flavors.

This is one of those dishes I had as a kid and had forgotten about until I was watching television and saw someone making it. The memories flooded back, and I rushed into the kitchen to make my own. Now, it's my husband and son's favorite dessert—my son even asks for it instead of birthday cake.

MAKES 10 TO 12 SERVINGS

Vegetable oil, for greasing
3 eggs
1¼ cups granulated sugar
½ cup unsalted butter, melted
4 tablespoons all-purpose flour
1 cup buttermilk

1 tablespoon lemon juice
2 teaspoons vanilla extract
⅛ teaspoon ground nutmeg
1 (9-inch) refrigerated store-bought
   pie crust

◆ Preheat the oven to 325 degrees F. Lightly grease a 9-inch pie pan.

◆ In a large mixing bowl, beat the eggs. Add in the sugar, butter, and flour. Mix until everything is well incorporated. Pour in the buttermilk and stir. Add the lemon juice, vanilla, and nutmeg. Mix until everything is nice and creamy.

◆ Pour the mixture into the pie shell, place it in the pie pan, and bake in the oven for 1 hour and 10 minutes, or until the filling is set. Let cool completely, for about 45 minutes, before cutting and serving.

Buttermilk Chocolate Cake

My grandma made chocolate cake that people in my family still talk about, even though she's been gone for more than three decades. But somehow, even though it was her most popular recipe, it never got passed down. So instead of using hers, I've had to make up my own version to keep the tradition going.

I happen to think that the best way to make chocolate cake is with hot coffee in the batter—the two flavors are a match made in heaven! I won't make a chocolate cake without it. Y'all also know I am adamant that I don't do dry cakes, so there's buttermilk in there to give it a little boost in flavor and texture. This cake is a simple sheet cake, so it's easy to take to family functions—just cover with aluminum foil or a lid.

MAKES 12 SERVINGS

½ cup vegetable oil, plus more
  for greasing
2 cups all-purpose flour, plus more
  for flouring
¾ cup unsweetened cocoa powder
2 teaspoons baking powder
1½ teaspoons baking soda
1 teaspoon kosher salt
2 cups granulated sugar
1 cup whole buttermilk
2 large eggs

1 tablespoon vanilla extract
1 cup hot coffee

For the frosting:
1½ cups (3 sticks) unsalted butter,
  at room temperature
5 cups powdered sugar
1 cup unsweetened cocoa powder
¼ cup coffee, at room temperature
¼ cup half-and-half
2 teaspoons vanilla extract

◆ Preheat the oven to 350 degrees F. Lightly grease and flour a 9-by-13-inch baking dish.

◆ Sift the flour into a large bowl along with the cocoa powder, baking powder, baking soda, and salt. Pour in the sugar, buttermilk, oil, eggs, and vanilla. Mix the ingredients with a handheld mixer at medium speed. Slowly start adding in the coffee. Mix on low speed until the ingredients are well combined.

◆ Pour the cake batter into the prepared baking dish and bake the cake for 30 to 35 minutes (or until done). Remove the cake from the oven and let cool.

- While the cake is cooling, prepare the frosting. Cream the butter using a handheld mixer on medium speed. Turn the mixer down to low speed, and slowly add the sugar and cocoa powder. Mix until well combined.

- Pour in the coffee and half-and-half and mix until nice and smooth. Next, add in the vanilla and continue to mix until the frosting is nice and creamy. Once the cake is completely cool, frost the cake.

Church Lady Lemon Coconut Pound Cake

◇◇

My aunt Nisha is like my second mom, and some Sundays she would bring me to her church. After service, they would have a dinner, and the desserts they served were all I could think about. Table after table filled with giant cakes, stacks of cookies, and sweet treats of all sorts. I always went straight for the best pound cake in the world—these ladies could have put the top bakeries in town to shame. My favorite was always the lemon coconut. This recipe is my homage to the masterful women behind the dessert table at my aunt Nisha's church.

MAKES 10 SERVINGS

Vegetable oil, for greasing
3 cups all-purpose flour, plus more for flouring
1 pound (4 sticks) salted butter, at room temperature
8 ounces cream cheese, at room temperature
3 cups granulated sugar
6 eggs
4 ounces instant lemon pudding mix

¼ cup sweetened shredded coconut
3 tablespoons lemon juice
Zest from 2 large lemons
2½ teaspoons coconut extract
2 teaspoons vanilla extract

For the glaze:
1½ cups powdered sugar
3 to 4 tablespoons lemon juice
1 teaspoon coconut extract

◆ Preheat the oven to 325 degrees F. Grease and flour a Bundt pan.

◆ In a stand mixer or large mixing bowl with a handheld mixer, cream the butter and cream cheese together at medium speed for about 2 to 3 minutes. Add in the sugar and start adding in the eggs. Mix on medium speed until well combined.

◆ Slowly add the flour, just a little at a time. Then add the pudding mix, shredded coconut, lemon juice and zest, coconut extract, and vanilla. Mix the batter on medium speed until it's creamy.

◆ Pour the cake batter into the prepared pan. Bake for 1 hour and 25 minutes, or until done. Remove the cake from the oven, and let it cool before removing it from the pan.

◆ While the cake cools, prepare the glaze. In a medium bowl, combine the powdered sugar, lemon juice, and coconut extract, and mix with a whisk until lump-free. Drizzle the glaze all over the cake, then let sit for 5 minutes before serving.

Sweet Potato Sponge Cake

<><><><><><><><><><><><><><><><><><><><><><><><><><><><><><><>

I don't usually love sponge cakes, because they're often a little dry for me. So when I wanted to make my own recipe, I needed to do something different. For this one, I use sweet potatoes the way some bakers use applesauce—the potatoes add tons of moisture but not much flavor (they do add a little color, though, which is fun). The result is so good that I ended up formulating it to make two at a time because it always goes so fast. To serve them, I just sprinkle them with a little powdered sugar before I put them out.

MAKES 16 SERVINGS

6 eggs at room temperature	½ teaspoon baking powder
1 cup granulated sugar	¼ teaspoon kosher salt
1 cup plus 1 tablespoon all-purpose flour	3 tablespoons mashed sweet potatoes
	1 teaspoon vanilla extract

- ◆ Preheat the oven to 350 degrees F. Spray two 9-inch cake pans with baking spray, or grease and flour them.

- ◆ In a large mixing bowl, beat the eggs with a handheld mixer on high speed for 1 to 2 minutes. Slowly start adding in the sugar, and continue to beat the eggs until they thicken and are nice and fluffy, about 5 minutes.

- ◆ In a medium bowl, combine the flour, baking powder, and salt. Whisk together until well incorporated. Set the bowl to the side.

- ◆ Add the mashed sweet potatoes and vanilla into the bowl with the fluffy eggs and stir, then sprinkle in the flour mixture. Slowly fold the ingredients until well incorporated, but don't overmix.

- ◆ Pour the cake batter evenly into each cake pan. Bake for 25 to 30 minutes. Remove from the oven and place the pans upside down on wire racks. Let cool for 5 minutes before removing the cakes from the pans, then let the cakes cool completely before serving.

Praline Bundt Cake

I'm a huge fan of praline anything, but this recipe doubles up on that Southern flavor by folding the pralines into an icing and drizzling it over pound cake. It's loaded with sugar and incredibly moist and basically just screams holiday season to me—probably because I can't make it more than once a year or I'd be in real trouble because I love it so much.

Remember, in this recipe—and all cakes—you never want to overmix the batter. That's how you get dry, dense cakes! Just use a low or medium speed on the mixer, and mix only until things are just combined or reach the texture instructed in the recipe.

MAKES 12 SERVINGS

3 cups all-purpose flour
1 teaspoon baking soda
1 teaspoon kosher salt
1½ cups brown sugar
1½ cups granulated sugar
1½ cups (3 sticks) unsalted butter,
   at room temperature
5 large eggs
1 cup buttermilk
1 tablespoon vanilla extract

For the icing:
5 tablespoons unsalted butter
1 cup brown sugar
1¼ cups powdered sugar
¼ cup evaporated milk
1 teaspoon vanilla extract
1 cup chopped pecans

◆ Preheat the oven to 325 degrees F. Spray a large Bundt pan with nonstick cooking spray.

◆ In a large mixing bowl, sift the flour, baking soda, and salt together. Set to the side.

◆ In a separate large bowl, combine the sugars and unsalted butter. Mix until it's nice and creamy, then start adding in the eggs one at a time. Mix until well combined.

◆ Alternate adding the buttermilk and the dry ingredients into the bowl with the butter-and-egg mixture until everything is in. Be sure to mix on low speed. Next, add the vanilla and fold into the batter.

- Pour the cake batter into the prepared pan and shake to get rid of any air pockets. Bake the cake for 1 hour to 1 hour and 15 minutes, until it's golden brown. Remove from the oven and let cool in the pan for 20 minutes before removing the cake from the pan.

- To make the icing, melt the butter in a medium saucepan over medium-high heat. Add in the brown sugar and powdered sugar. Pour in the evaporated milk, and stir. Let bubble for 2 minutes, then turn off the heat. Add in the vanilla and sprinkle in the pecans. Fold in the ingredients, then let sit for 20 minutes.

- Pour the pecan icing all over the cake, and let the cake stand for at least 30 minutes before serving.

Pineapple Upside-Down Cheesecake

I was that kid in my family—you know, the one that would go around while everyone was busy talking and pinch little pieces off all the cakes on the dessert table. And there was nothing I liked to pinch more than my aunt Nisha's pineapple upside-down cake. Well, one Christmas I was doing just that when my grandpa caught me! I froze at first, thinking I was in for it—but then I realized he was there because he was busy pinching cheesecake. I like to think of this pineapple upside-down cheesecake as the result of that day, a combination of our little secret pinches. This recipe is adapted from one I saw on Delish a while back.

MAKES 12 SERVINGS

For the cakes:

⅓ cup vegetable oil, plus more for greasing

4 tablespoons unsalted butter, melted

½ cup dark brown sugar

1 (20-ounce) can pineapple rings, in juice

10 to 12 Maraschino cherries

1 (15.25-ounce) package of yellow cake mix

1 cup crushed pineapple

3 large eggs, lightly beaten

For the filling:

24 ounces cream cheese, softened

1 cup powdered sugar

¼ cup sour cream

3 eggs

2 tablespoons all-purpose flour

1 tablespoon vanilla extract

1 tablespoon pineapple juice

◆ Preheat the oven to 350 degrees F. Lightly oil two 8-inch springform pans. Set one aside, and add the melted butter and brown sugar to the other. Add the pineapple rings to the bottom of the pan, then add the Maraschino cherries in the center of the pineapple rings. Place the springform pan to the side.

◆ Empty the cake mix into a large mixing bowl and whisk out the lumps. Add in the crushed pineapple, vegetable oil, and eggs. Mix until well combined.

CONTINUED

- Divide the batter, and pour half over the pineapple, cherry, and brown sugar mixture. Pour the remaining batter into the second springform pan. Bake the cakes for 25 to 30 minutes, or until done. Let the cakes cool.

- In a large mixing bowl, combine the cream cheese, powdered sugar, and sour cream. Mix until it's nice and creamy, then start adding in the eggs. Add the flour, vanilla, and pineapple juice. Mix until well combined.

- Pour the cheesecake filling over the cakes in the springform pans. Wrap the bottom of the pans with aluminum foil, and place them into a roasting pan. Create a water bath by pouring about 2 to 3 inches of hot water into the roasting pan.

- Place the cakes in the oven, and bake for 1 hour to 1 hour and 15 minutes, until the filling is set. It should jiggle a tad, like Jell-O. Let cool. Remove the cakes from the springform pans. Place the cake with the pineapples and cherries on top of the cheesecake layer. Let sit for 10 minutes before serving.

Mom's Rice Pudding

My mom would sometimes make rice pudding for a special treat for me because something about the rice, cream, and cinnamon just spoke comfort. And actually, that hasn't really changed much at all, except that now that I make it myself, I can tweak it perfectly to my tastes. A little more vanilla here, a little bit fewer raisins there. I add a dash of nutmeg because it brightens everything. But most importantly, I use half-and-half, which produces the creamiest rice pudding, which my mom could never even have imagined.

MAKES 4 TO 6 SERVINGS

2 cups half-and-half, divided	2 teaspoons vanilla extract
1½ cups cooked rice	½ teaspoon ground cinnamon
2 tablespoons unsalted butter	½ teaspoon kosher salt
1 egg	¼ teaspoon ground nutmeg
⅓ cup granulated sugar	¼ cup raisins

◆ In a medium saucepan over medium heat, combine 1½ cups of the half-and-half with the cooked rice and butter. Stir the ingredients, and simmer for 15 minutes.

◆ While that's cooking, combine the remaining half-and-half with the egg, sugar, vanilla, cinnamon, salt, and nutmeg in a medium bowl. Mix until well combined.

◆ After the rice mixture has been cooking for 15 minutes, pour in the egg mixture and raisins and stir. Cook over medium heat for 5 minutes. Turn the heat off and stir the ingredients. Serve warm or cold.

Fancy Banana Pudding

◇◇◇

My grandmother made the best banana pudding, according to my cousins, aunts, uncles, and mom. Sadly, I never got my hands on the recipe, but I like to think that when I make this, I'm channeling a little bit of Grandma. Several family members say this tastes pretty close to my grandma's, which is the highest compliment I can imagine.

I consider this one to be my "fancy" banana pudding—you know I've made a ton of different kinds. But this one uses real bananas, and everything is made from scratch—except for the cookies, of course. Vanilla wafers are the classic here, but I had a reader suggest switching out half the wafers with Chessmen cookies, and since this is the fancy version, I gave it a try—it works, and it looks great too.

MAKES 8 TO 10 SERVINGS

1 cup granulated sugar	2 teaspoons vanilla extract
⅓ cup cornstarch	1½ cups heavy cream
½ teaspoon kosher salt	⅔ cup powdered sugar, sifted
¼ teaspoon ground nutmeg	4 large ripe bananas
3 cups whole milk	1 (11-ounce) box vanilla wafers
3 eggs	1 package of Chessmen cookies

◆ In a large saucepan, combine the sugar, cornstarch, salt, and nutmeg. Sift or stir the ingredients, then pour in the milk and stir until well combined. Place the pan over medium heat and cook for about 15 minutes. Stir continuously. Reduce the heat to low and scoop out about ½ cup of the hot milk mixture.

◆ In a large bowl, beat the eggs. Slowly pour in the ½ cup of the hot milk mixture and continue to stir. By doing this, you are slowly bringing the eggs up to temperature, and this prevents the eggs from cooking when you add them to the saucepan.

- Return to the stove top and turn the heat back to medium. Stir the hot milk mixture and add the egg mixture into the saucepan. Stir continuously and add in the vanilla. Stir and cook for an additional 2 minutes. Remove from the heat and let it sit for 2 minutes. Pour the hot pudding into a heat-resistant bowl.

- Once the pudding has cooled slightly, cover it with plastic wrap. Make sure that the plastic wrap is touching the pudding. This prevents the pudding from forming a film on top. Let the pudding sit until it reaches room temperature.

- While the pudding cools, prepare the whipped cream. Pour the heavy cream into a medium bowl and sprinkle in the powdered sugar. Mix the ingredients with a hand-held mixer on high speed until it turns into whipped cream. Set the bowl to the side.

- Once the pudding has reached room temperature, slice up the bananas.

- In a 9-by-13-inch baking dish, add some vanilla wafers and banana slices on the bottom, then add half of the pudding on top. Smooth out the layer of pudding, then add another layer of wafers and bananas. Add the final layer of pudding, then add the whipped cream. Top the pudding with the Chessmen cookies and serve. Cover and refrigerate any leftovers.

Pralines

◇◇◇

Pralines have to be one of my all-time favorite candies. We called them pecan candy growing up, and my aunts always made them for us. For whatever reason, a lot of people think that they have to buy pralines—they're heading to New Orleans and pick them up as a souvenir. But you don't have to wait for a trip! You can make your very own pralines at home for a fraction of the price, and they'll taste even better!

MAKES 9 SERVINGS

1¼ cups granulated sugar
1 cup light brown sugar
7 tablespoons salted butter
½ cup half-and-half
1 tablespoon vanilla extract
1½ cups chopped pecans

- In a large saucepan over medium heat, combine the sugars, butter, and half-and-half. Bring the candy mixture to 240 degrees F, and let it boil for about 5 minutes without stirring.

- After the 5 minutes, add in the vanilla and stir. Remove from the heat. Toss in the pecans and fold in with a wooden spoon. Continue to stir the candy mixture until it thickens.

- Spoon out the candy mixture onto parchment paper. Let the candy cool completely before enjoying.

A Little Something to Sip

Sweet Tea

<><><><><><><><><><><><><><><><><><><><><><><><><><><><><><><><>

Sweet tea is like water in Baton Rouge—if you're thirsty, they're going to bring you a big glass of sweet tea. At every meal, the tables will be set with big plastic dispensers of it on the table, and there's always more in the fridge, gallons and gallons of it. And nobody in my family is going to drink unsweetened ice tea. The trick to keeping it from getting bitter is that little pinch of baking soda so that it's perfect for serving up ice cold with lemon slices.

MAKES 16 SERVINGS

---

1 gallon boiling water
3 family-size black tea bags
2½ cups granulated sugar
¼ teaspoon baking soda
Mint leaves, for garnish

◆ Pour the hot water into a pitcher, then add in the tea bags. Let the tea bags sit for 15 to 20 minutes, then remove.

◆ Pour in the sugar and baking soda. Stir until the sugar and baking soda dissolve.

◆ Cover the tea and refrigerate until it's nice and cold, about 2 hours. Garnish with mint before serving.

Fresh-Squeezed Lemonade

◇◇

The second most important drink to sweet tea in the soul food universe is lemonade, and I mean the real stuff, made with actual freshly squeezed lemons, water, and sugar. I know lots of people like the bottled and powdered stuff, and sometimes I drink that too, but I just can't even think of it as lemonade. That's some other drink, and this here is lemonade—and it isn't that much harder to make than opening a bottle.

MAKES 8 SERVINGS

Juice from 8 large lemons
6 cups water
1¼ cups granulated sugar
1 lemon, sliced (optional)

- In a large pitcher, combine the lemon juice with the water and sugar. Stir until the sugar is dissolved. Refrigerate until cold, about 1 hour.

- Pour the lemonade over ice, and add a lemon slice to each glass before serving.

Blackberry Wine Slushies

You can barely go for a walk in Seattle in late summer or early fall without stumbling on a thicket of blackberries, so I use them for everything—they're just free on the side of every road! One day I was out picking them to make a blackberry pie, but when I got home, cousins, I was just tired. I didn't want to make a pie, I wanted a drink. So I hatched a better plan for those lovely berries. By the time the berries were frozen, I'd invited a few girlfriends over, and I had just the drink to serve them. They did not miss the pie.

MAKES 6 SERVINGS

3 cups frozen blackberries
1 (750–milliliter) bottle Arbor Mist
    Blackberry Merlot
¼ cup powdered sugar
Mint leaves, for garnish

◆ Place the blackberries into a blender and pour in the merlot. Sprinkle in the powdered sugar. Blend everything until it's nice and smooth. Garnish with mint.

Citrus Sangria

◇◇◇

You can just call this gossip juice. My girlfriends know that when they're coming over to binge on some Netflix shows or something, I'll have a pitcher of this waiting in the fridge. It takes about two hours of chilling for the flavors to really come together, but when they do, it is so easy to drink. Then when my friends get here and we have a few glasses, suddenly hours will go by and we will be all caught up on each other's lives—and everyone else's too, you know!

MAKES 4 TO 6 SERVINGS

1 (750-milliliter) bottle sweet moscato
1½ cups pineapple juice
1 cup white rum
1 cup pineapple chunks
2 limes, sliced
2 oranges, sliced

◆ Combine all the ingredients into a pitcher and stir. Refrigerate for a minimum of 2 hours before serving.

Watermelon Margaritas

◇◇

The margarita is my signature drink, and I love all flavored margaritas, but the Watermelon Margarita is special because it has a nice light flavor that pairs so well with the tequila. The trick to this recipe is to prepare the watermelon ahead of time by cubing and freezing it. Then you can toss it into the blender for a slushy drink without adding the extra water from ice cubes.

MAKES 4 TO 6 SERVINGS

2 cups water

1 cup granulated sugar

1½ cups freshly squeezed lime juice
   (from about 12 limes)

8 cups seedless watermelon
   cubes, frozen

1 cup silver tequila

½ cup triple sec

Coarse salt, for rims

Watermelon slices, for serving

Lime wedges, for serving

◆ In a medium saucepan over medium heat, combine the water, sugar, and lime juice. Stir until the sugar is completely dissolved. Turn the heat off and let the syrup cool.

◆ Add the cooled syrup, watermelon, tequila, and triple sec to a blender. Blend until everything is nice and smooth.

◆ Wet the rims of your glasses, then salt them. Pour the margaritas and add a lime wedge and watermelon slice to each of the glasses before serving.

Pineapple Mimosas

<><><><><><><><><><><><><><><><><><><><><><><><><><><>

You know if I find something boring, I'm going to find a way to dress it up. And regular mimosas just are not that exciting to me. So I had to switch most of the orange juice out for pineapple, and now it's tart, a little sweeter, and so very tropical. You better believe it tastes like paradise!

MAKES 4 TO 6 SERVINGS

1 (750–milliliter) bottle sparkling
   white wine
2 cups pineapple juice
½ cup orange juice
Orange slices, for serving
Pineapple slices, for serving

◆ Combine the sparkling white wine, pineapple juice, and orange juice. Stir until well combined.

◆ Fill the champagne glasses and add fruit slices on the rims before serving.

Spiked Fruit Punch

◇◇◇

The other name for this is "Grown Folks' Punch," because this was the punch that all the aunts and uncles hid in the back of the fridge during family gatherings so the kids wouldn't get into it. They even used different color cups from the kids so nobody would accidentally get into the wrong version—because the truth is, it doesn't look or taste too much different from kids' punch, and that can spell trouble.

MAKES 10 TO 12 SERVINGS

6 cups fruit punch
3 cups pineapple juice
2 cups peach schnapps
2 cups white rum
1 cup lemon-lime soda
¼ cup lime juice
2 small limes, sliced and frozen
1 large orange, sliced and frozen

◆ Combine the fruit punch, pineapple juice, peach schnapps, rum, soda, and lime juice into a large pitcher. Stir until well combined, then cover and refrigerate until nice and cold.

◆ Pour the fruit punch into a large punch bowl, then add in the frozen fruit. Serve and enjoy!

Acknowledgments

Shout-out to my mom, Suzanne, and her sisters, Nisha, Deborah, Frances, Rosemary, and Josie, for allowing me in their kitchens when I was a child and teaching me the basics.

Special thanks to my uncle Eddie and cousin TJ.

Leigh Eisenman, thank you for taking me on. I appreciate you!

Also I'd like to thank Angie Thomas—thanks for *everything*.

MENUS

◇◇◇◇◇◇◇◇◇◇◇◇◇

Soul Food Brunch

Family Picnic

Sunday Supper

Southern-Style Finger-Food Football Party

INDEX

◇◇◇◇◇◇◇◇◇◇◇◇◇◇

Note: Page numbers in *italic* refer to photographs.

CONVERSIONS

◇◇◇◇◇◇◇◇◇◇◇◇◇◇◇◇◇◇◇◇◇◇◇◇◇◇◇◇◇◇◇◇◇

VOLUME

UNITED STATES	METRIC	IMPERIAL
¼ tsp.	1.25 ml	
½ tsp.	2.5 ml	
1 tsp.	5 ml	
½ Tbsp.	7.5 ml	
1 Tbsp.	15 ml	
⅛ c.	30 ml	1 fl. oz.
¼ c.	60 ml	2 fl. oz.
⅓ c.	80 ml	2.5 fl. oz.
½ c.	125 ml	4 fl. oz.
1 c.	250 ml	8 fl. oz.
2 c. (1 pt.)	500 ml	16 fl. oz.
1 qt.	1 l	32 fl. oz.

LENGTH

UNITED STATES	METRIC
⅛ in.	3 mm
¼ in.	6 mm
½ in.	1.25 cm
1 in.	2.5 cm
1 ft.	30 cm

WEIGHT

AVOIRDUPOIS	METRIC
¼ oz.	7 g
½ oz.	15 g
1 oz.	30 g
2 oz.	60 g
3 oz.	90 g
4 oz.	115 g
5 oz.	150 g
6 oz.	175 g
7 oz.	200 g
8 oz. (½ lb.)	225 g
9 oz.	250 g
10 oz.	300 g
11 oz.	325 g
12 oz.	350 g
13 oz.	375 g
14 oz.	400 g
15 oz.	425 g
16 oz. (1 lb.)	450 g
1½ lb.	750 g
2 lb.	900 g
2¼ lb.	1 kg
3 lb.	1.4 kg
4 lb.	1.8 kg

TEMPERATURE

OVEN MARK	FAHRENHEIT	CELSIUS	GAS
Very cool	250–275	130–140	½–1
Cool	300	150	2
Warm	325	165	3
Moderate	350	175	4
Moderately hot	375	190	5
	400	200	6
Hot	425	220	7
	450	230	8
Very Hot	475	245	9

Printed in China

SASQUATCH BOOKS with colophon is a registered trademark of Penguin Random House LLC

24 23 22 21 20   9 8 7 6 5 4 3 2 1

Editors: Hannah Elnan, Susan Roxborough
Designer: Anna Goldstein
Photographs: Michael Kartes
Food and prop styling: Danielle Kartes

Library of Congress Cataloging-in-Publication Data

Names: Mayes, Rosie (Food writer), author. | Kartes, Danielle, photographer
   (expression) | Kartes, Michael, photographer (expression)
Title: I heart soul food : 100 Southern comfort food favorites / Rosie
   Mayes ; photography by Danielle and Michael Kartes.
Description: Seattle : Sasquatch Books, 2020. | Includes index.
Identifiers: LCCN 2019052779 (print) | LCCN 2019052780 (ebook) | ISBN
   9781632173096 (paperback) | ISBN 9781632173102 (ebook)
Subjects: LCSH: African American cooking. | Cooking, American–Southern
   style. | Comfort food–Southern States. | LCGFT: Cookbooks.
Classification: LCC TX715.2.A47 M39 2020 (print) | LCC TX715.2.A47
   (ebook) | DDC 641.59/296073–dc23
LC record available at https://lccn.loc.gov/2019052779
LC ebook record available at https://lccn.loc.gov/2019052780

ISBN: 978-1-63217-309-6

Sasquatch Books
1904 Third Avenue, Suite 710
Seattle, WA 98101

SasquatchBooks.com